W9-BUZ-012

WITHDRAWN

The Supreme Court and the Commander in Chief

Da Capo Press Reprints in

AMERICAN CONSTITUTIONAL AND LEGAL HISTORY

GENERAL EDITOR: LEONARD W. LEVY
Brandeis University

The Supreme Court and the Commander in Chief

BY CLINTON ROSSITER

DA CAPO PRESS · NEW YORK · 1970

A Da Capo Press Reprint Edition

Library of Congress Catalog Card Number 76-98182
SBN 306-71832-4

Copyright 1951 by Cornell University

Published by Da Capo Press
A Division of Plenum Publishing Corporation
227 West 17th Street
New York, N. Y. 10011
All Rights Reserved

Manufactured in the United States of America

The Supreme Court and

the Commander in Chief

The Supreme Court and the Commander in Chief

CLINTON ROSSITER *Cornell University*

Cornell University Press ITHACA, NEW YORK

To a gentle friend and ideal colleague

ELIAS HUZAR, 1915-1950

Preface

LIKE most students of the government of the United States, I have observed with interest the varied and delicate relationships among its three great independent branches. I have often thought that the true study of our system of government begins with these points of contact —between President and Congress, Congress and Supreme Court, and Supreme Court and President—rather than with the powers and functions of any one of the three branches.

This study is directed to the third of these relationships. It attempts to show how the Supreme Court, in deciding several hundred cases involving the scope of the national war powers, has interpreted the President's status and authority as commander in chief. Perhaps it should bear the title "The Supreme Court and the War Powers of the United States," but the figure of the President looms so large—in the use of these powers and in their interpretation at the hands of the Court—that I feel safe in treating this problem as one important strand in the nexus of relationships between the executive and judicial organs of our uniquely three-part government. In any case, this is a limited study of a limited aspect of one of our three fundamental intragovernmental relationships. I trust my readers will bear this fact in mind.

I am indebted for aid and comfort to my two distinguished friends and teachers, Edward S. Corwin of
Princeton and Robert E. Cushman of Cornell, and to my
excellent contemporaries, John P. Roche of Haverford and
T. L. Tolan, Jr., of the Milwaukee Bar. Miss Shirley Ford
of Van Etten, New York, has been the best of all possible
typists. And after the silence of two former prefaces in
which I was forbidden to mention her name, I am now
permitted to acknowledge that my wife, Mary Crane
Rossiter, has taught me all I know about grammar, style,
and taste.

CLINTON ROSSITER

Ithaca, New York
October, 1950

Contents

The Supreme Court and

the Commander in Chief

Introduction

WARS and rumors of war have set us to thinking about
the shape of the national government in an atomic catas-
trophe. There is much talk of *power*, and thus of the final
power of national self-preservation in the American constitutional system: the immense authority of the President
as commander in chief. There is little talk of *limitations*,
of the techniques through which the uses of this authority
can be confined to paths of constitutional righteousness.
We seem grimly prepared to submit to strong and arbitrary government in the event of atomic attack, but we
avoid consideration of the methods through which we can
render such government trustworthy and temporary.[1]

On the assumption that it is never too late, even in an
age of vast sociopolitical flux, to speak of constitutional
limitations, this book examines the operation of one order
of restraint upon presidential power in which millions of
Americans continue to put their special trust. More specifically, it relates the "natural history" of the Supreme
Court's role as overseer and interpreter of the war powers,
especially the power of the President as commander in

[1] See generally Clinton Rossiter, "Constitutional Dictatorship in
the Atomic Age," *Review of Politics,* XI (1949), 395–418, and
references there cited.

chief. These are the questions for which it seeks answers: What use has the Court, whether under Taney or Chase or White or Stone, made of its opportunities to speak with authority on this most awful of presidential powers? When has it been bold, when silent amid the clash of arms? Under what circumstances have Court and President met in head-on disagreement, and what effect upon the latter's course of action did the censures of the judiciary actually have? What permanent influence on the extent and content of the war powers has been worked by the Court's decisions? What future trust can we place in the Court as defender of constitutionalism in time of great national crisis? In fine, the purpose of this book is to evaluate the effectiveness of the momentous American doctrine of judicial review in an area of presidential-military power that may well hold our future in its flexible grasp. It is a study in the realities of constitutional law.

In exercising his lofty prerogatives as "Commander in Chief of the Army and Navy of the United States" the President would seem to enjoy a peculiar degree of freedom from the review and restraints of the judicial process. His powers in the broad field of national defense are largely discretionary, and the exercise of military discretion is one species of official action that American courts have always held themselves particularly unqualified to control. The recruiting and training of personnel, the stationing of troops in peace and their deployment in war, the appointment and removal of "high brass," the selection of corporations with which to let contracts for matériel, the determination to buy more B-36's and halt work on ultramodern carriers, the decisions on when and how fast to produce atomic bombs and where and when

2

to use them—these are matters over which no court would or could exercise the slightest measure of judgment or restraint. For his conduct of such affairs the President is responsible, so far as he can be held responsible, only to Congress, the electorate, and the pages of history. It would seem at first sight that the Supreme Court could do nothing to control or even interpret the President's authority to command the forces and wage war, and that the war powers would therefore have no judicial history.

Yet the 340-odd volumes of the *United States Reports* are crammed with cases familiar to all students of American government—*Martin v. Mott,* the *Prize Cases, Ex parte Milligan, Arver v. United States, Korematsu v. United States,* to mention a few of the more notable—in which some element of the President's military competence was directly before a Court that was constitutionally and often practically in a position to restrain the free play of his martial will. The war powers of the United States, especially as brought to bear by the commander in chief, can play hob with personal and property rights, and a number of injured individuals have had enough determination and resources to push their cases through to the highest level, and thus to force the Supreme Court to examine critically some of the most high-toned of the military powers of President and Congress. A passing glance at such volumes as 7 *Wallace* or 321 *U.S.* will demonstrate the amazing number of cases in which the legality of the government's interference with private or property rights was sufficiently dubious to permit close judicial scrutiny. Lincoln could not be challenged in court for placing Ambrose E. Burnside in command of the Army of the Potomac, but his blockade of the South, suspension of

3

the writ of habeas corpus, and trial of civilians by military commission were all put to judicial test. Roosevelt gave no thought to the Supreme Court in deciding when and where to invade Europe, but he, i.e., his Attorney General, thought long and hard (and not too well) about the constitutionality of the evacuation of the west coast Japanese-Americans and the seizure of Montgomery Ward. And he, too, was challenged seriously on four or five major exertions of his martial powers.

The first part of this study examines the Court's construction of the President's power of martial rule, of all his powers the most basic, spectacular, and injurious to private rights. The second deals with five other problems arising under the war powers on which the Court has discoursed with varied results for presidential authority. By way of introduction to the whole subject, we shall reverse the usual procedure in such matters and establish at the outset a number of general propositions concerning the Court's historic attitude toward the President's war powers. In mounting the attack upon the specific from a solid base of generality, we should be better prepared to follow the twists and turns of the Court's opinions. A long and painstaking consideration of the hundreds of important cases in which the Court has declaimed on the Constitution-at-war would appear to lead to these conclusions:

First, the Court has refused to speak about the powers of the President as commander in chief in any but the most guarded terms. It has been respectful, complimentary, on occasion properly awed, but it has never embarked on one of those expansive flights of dicta into which it has been so often tempted by other great constitutional questions.

4

It has moved well beyond the limited concepts of Hamilton in *The Federalist*, number 69 ("It would amount to nothing more than the supreme command and direction of the military and naval forces, as first General and admiral of the Confederacy"), and of Taney in *Fleming v. Page* ("His duty and his power are purely military"),[2] but not nearly so far as have the Presidents themselves. The breath-taking estimates of their war powers announced and acted upon by Lincoln and Roosevelt have earned no blessing under the hands of the judiciary.

Second, the pronouncements of the Court have been as general as they have been guarded. It has fixed neither the outer boundaries nor the inner divisions of the President's martial authority, and has failed completely to draw the line between his powers and those of Congress,[3] except to proclaim such self-evident dogmas as that Congress cannot direct campaigns nor the President declare war. The thinking of the Court on this point was best expressed by Justice Swayne in *Stewart v. Kahn:* "The measures to be taken in carrying on war and to suppress insurrection are not defined. The decision of all questions rests wholly in the discretion of those to whom the substantial powers involved are confided by the Constitution."[4] It is apparently for the President, not the Court, to be specific about his powers.

Third, the Court's estimate of its ability to intervene in an improper exercise of the war powers has been one thing at one time, another at another. Often in one period,

[2] 9 Howard 603, 615 (1850). See also *U.S. v. Sweeny*, 157 U.S. 281, 284 (1895).

[3] See Taney's inadequate attempt in his concurring opinion in *Ex parte Milligan*, 4 Wallace 2, 139–140 (1866).

[4] 11 Wallace 493, 506 (1870).

or even in one case, its attitude has been quite ambivalent. Counsel for injured interests can always quote an overpowering and apparently conclusive array of decisions and dicta proving that the Court will actively defend the Constitution against the havoc of war; but the government's lawyers can come right back with an equally impressive array, plucked in many instances from the very same cases, proving the incapacity of the Court to put a bridle on the war powers. Of course, by now almost all great constitutional problems have respectable lines of precedents on both sides, as the present Court reminds us repeatedly with its split decisions. Yet in this area of the war powers it is particularly striking how unsure the Court has been about its real or nominal authority to substitute its judgment for that of Congress, the President, or his military subordinates. This unsettling fact will become especially evident in the analysis of the opinions in *Duncan v. Kahanamoku* and *Korematsu v. United States*.[5]

Fourth, the Court has made it a practice never to approve a challenged presidential or military order solely on the authority of the commander-in-chief clause if it can find a more specific and less controversial basis. The judges, that is to say, will do everything in their power to avoid considering an unusual action in terms of the President's power alone, and will seize with manifest relief on any evidence of congressional approval. In the outstanding cases to arise from the recent war there are dozens of remarks such as, "We have no occasion to consider whether the President, acting alone, could lawfully have made the curfew order in question," or, "It is unnecessary for present purposes to determine to what ex-

[5] Below, pp. 48–59.

tent the President as Commander in Chief has constitutional power to create military commissions without the support of Congressional legislation" [6]—each followed by reference to some act of Congress that could be cited in support of the President's extraordinary action. This preference for statutory over constitutional authority actually works to the President's advantage, for the merger of his military powers and those of Congress produces something known simply but grandly as "the war powers of the United States," under which just about any presidential wartime action can be brought within the limits of the Constitution. Both President and Congress have constitutional powers of their own in military and foreign affairs; when these powers are merged they are virtually irresistible, at least in the courts. This is one instance in which two plus two equals five. And the powers, of course, are his to wield.

Finally, the Court has usually been quite realistic about the constitutional ability of this nation, led by its President, to wage war. There have been several occasions, as in the post-Civil War case *Ex parte Milligan*, on which it has been lured into saying things about limits on the war powers that were simply not true. For the most part, however, it has agreed with Chief Justice Hughes's famous observations that "the war power of the Federal Government . . . is a power to wage war successfully" and that "so, also, we have a *fighting* constitution." [7] This does not

[6] *Hirabayashi v. U.S.*, 320 U.S. 81, 92 (1943); *Ex parte Quirin*, 317 U.S. 1, 29 (1942).

[7] *Home Building and Loan Association v. Blaisdell*, 290 U.S. 398, 426 (1934); "War Powers under the Constitution," *American Bar Association Reports*, XLII (1917), 238.

mean that the Constitution goes to pieces in the event of war, for, as Hughes also remarked, "While we are at war, we are not in revolution." [8] It does mean that the Court has recognized, always *bello flagrante* and almost always *post bellum,* the cogency of Hamilton's contention in *The Federalist,* number 23, that the war powers "ought to exist without limitation, *because it is impossible to foresee or define the extent and variety of national exigencies, or the correspondent extent and variety of the means which may be necessary to satisfy them.*"

In another post-Civil War case, *Miller v. United States,*[9] Justice Strong observed, "Of course the power to declare war involves the power to prosecute it by all means and in any manner in which war may be legitimately prosecuted." Just what he meant by "legitimately" he did not go on to say, but other opinions have made clear that the war powers must be wielded in accordance with the great qualifications found "in the Constitution or in applicable principles of international law." [10] Yet the latter is today simply a moral limitation, while the new view of the former, like so many new views simply an echo of Hamilton's illustrious voice, is that the Constitution encourages rather than discourages the use of the war powers. It has been fashionable among the justices in recent years to be a little more tough-minded, or simply resigned, on the nature and scope of these powers. The Constitution, said Justice Burton in a recent austere dissent,

[8] "War Powers under the Constitution," 232.

[9] 11 Wallace 268, 305 (1870).

[10] *U.S. v. Macintosh,* 283 U.S. 605, 622 (1931). See also *U.S. v. Russell,* 13 Wallace 623, 627 (1871); *Hamilton v. Kentucky Distilleries,* 251 U.S. 146, 155–156 (1919); *U.S. v. Cohen Grocery Co.,* 255 U.S. 81, 88–89 (1921).

8

was written by a generation fresh from war. The people established a more perfect union, in part, so that they might the better defend themselves from military attack. In doing so they centralized far more military power and responsibility in the Chief Executive than previously had been done. The Constitution was built for rough as well as smooth roads. In time of war the nation simply changes gears and takes the harder going under the same power.[11]

And his brother Frankfurter, some two years before:

The provisions of the Constitution which confer on the Congress and the President powers to enable this country to wage war are as much part of the Constitution as provisions looking to a nation at peace. . . . Therefore, the validity of action under the war power must be judged wholly in the context of war.[12]

At another point in the same opinion he protests against the timid, unrealistic concept of the war powers that would

suffuse a part of the Constitution with an atmosphere of unconstitutionality. . . . To recognize that military orders are "reasonably expedient military precautions" in time of war and yet to deny them constitutional legitimacy makes of the Constitution an instrument for dialectic subtleties not reasonably to be attributed to the hard-headed Framers, of whom a majority had had actual participation in war.[13]

And as a final touch, again Justice Burton:

Within their proper spheres, the robust strength and freedom of action allowed to the policy making and policy exe-

[11] *Duncan v. Kahanamoku*, 327 U.S. 304, 342 (1946).
[12] *Korematsu v. U.S.*, 323 U.S. 214, 224 (1944).
[13] 323 U.S. 214, 225.

cuting agencies of our Government are as vital to the success of our great experiment in securing "the Blessings of Liberty to ourselves and our Posterity" as are the checks and balances which have been imposed upon our representatives.[14]

[14] 327 U.S. 304, 338. Although the Court's interpretation of the President's powers in foreign affairs is outside the scope of this book, those two recent "realistic" cases, *U.S. v. Curtiss-Wright Export Corp.*, 299 U.S. 304 (1936), and *Lichter v. U.S.*, 334 U.S. 742 (1948), should be carefully noted as first cousins to the Burton-Frankfurter thesis.

PART I

The Supreme Court and the

President's Power of Martial Rule

AS commander in chief and chief executive the President
is empowered, indeed obliged, to preserve the peace of
the United States against domestic violence and alien
attack. The mandates of the Constitution, a procession of
statutes dating back to 1792,[1] and the logic of history and
political science have combined to place in his keeping a
virtually uncontrollable discretion in employing the armed
forces to defend the nation, execute the laws, and maintain national authority on every foot of American soil.
Although this is a presidential power equally serviceable
in peace and war, it is generally treated in the context
of the war powers because it derives the substance of its
authority from his status as commander in chief and because its most precedential uses have taken place in
periods of armed conflict, especially those of the Civil
War and World War II.

It is impossible to define with precision the scope of
what we have conveniently labeled "the President's power

[1] *United States Code*, Title 50, secs. 201–204. See also Hamilton's provident words in defense of "energy in the executive" in the
first paragraphs of *The Federalist*, number 70.

of martial rule," for it runs the gamut of military action from the mere threat of force to outright martial law. For the sake of convenience, his power may be broken down into three general, closely related categories: (1) *the power of martial law,* under which he may, with some show of formality, extend military government to domestic areas in case of invasion or rebellion; [2] (2) *the power simply to "call out the troops,"* which might involve anything from placing a platoon on a mail train moving through a strike-bound area to summoning the entire militia to preserve the Union; and, (3) *the power to suspend the writ of habeas corpus,* which may or may not accompany martial law, and which, as we shall shortly see, may or may not belong to the President!

Just where one of these powers leaves off and the other begins is something Presidents themselves would have trouble explaining. The uses of emergency powers have not been carefully institutionalized in this country, and Presidents like Washington, Lincoln, Cleveland, Wilson, and Franklin D. Roosevelt have wielded military force in time of crisis without much thought about the forms that their display of authority might assume. A major strike touched with violence, a wartime strike blocking the flow

[2] For a discussion of martial law, which is to be carefully distinguished from military law as well as military government of conquered areas, see Clinton Rossiter, *Constitutional Dictatorship* (Princeton, N.J., 1948), 9, 139–150, 215–217, and the many references there cited, especially Charles Fairman, *The Law of Martial Rule* (2d ed.; Chicago, 1943). In *U.S. v. Diekelman,* 92 U.S. 520, 526 (1875), Chief Justice Waite remarked, "Martial law is the law of military necessity in the actual presence of war. It is administered by the general of the army, and is in fact his will. Of necessity it is arbitrary; but it must be obeyed." For "general of the army" we may read "President."

of munitions, a great fire or flood accompanied by riots and looting, a localized rebellion with which the state authorities cannot cope, a major insurrection, the threat or actuality of alien invasion—all these are situations into which our armed forces have moved decisively under the direction and in the name of the President. In each instance it has been for the President himself to decide what type and degree of force was necessary to remedy the abnormal situation. As the exigencies of the emergency, the character of the incumbent, and the state of public opinion have varied, so, too, has the shape of the President's action.

Now it goes without saying that any such use of presidential power must inevitably interfere drastically with the normal exercise of private rights and civil liberties, whether those of a single person or a class or a particular area or the entire nation, and the courts have always been open—if not during the emergency, then at some later date—to hear the complaints of citizens unnecessarily restricted or too roughly handled by the forces acting under the President's direction. The Supreme Court has had occasion in about ten major cases to pass judgment on the President's military authority to circumscribe the normal liberties of the people in defense of the nation. Since judges have experienced just about as much difficulty as Presidents in defining with precision the boundaries and components of the power under scrutiny, we would be hard put to it to treat this subject any other way but chronologically. The plan, therefore, is to examine the decisions of the Court as they have followed one another in history.

The Element of Discretion:
Martin v. Mott and *Luther v. Borden*

Although the first seventy years under the Constitution were replete with emergencies calling for strong presidential action to preserve the peace—the Whiskey Rebellion, the Embargo troubles, the War of 1812, Nullification in South Carolina, the Mexican War, to name the most important—on only two occasions did the Supreme Court have a chance to say anything of note about martial rule, in the justly famed cases *Martin v. Mott* and *Luther v. Borden*.[3] Neither went to the root of the matter under present consideration, yet together they illustrate, and are still cited in support of, a fundamental principle of judicial review of the President's power of martial rule. Perhaps the best way to define this principle is to quote, with the aid of italics, the significant words of the two great judges who delivered these opinions.

Story for the Court in *Martin v. Mott* (1827):

The power thus confided by Congress to the President is doubtless of a very high and delicate nature. A free people are naturally very jealous of the exercise of military power; and the power to call the militia into actual service is certainly felt to be one of no ordinary magnitude. . . . It is, in its terms, a limited power, confined to cases of actual invasion, or of imminent danger of invasion. If it be a limited power, the question arises, by whom is the exigency to be judged of and decided? . . . *We are all of opinion that the authority to decide whether the exigency has arisen belongs exclusively to the President, and that his decision is conclusive upon all other persons.*

[3] 12 Wheaton 19, 29–33 (1827); 7 Howard 1, 42–45 (1849).

14

The law does not provide for any appeal from the judgment of the President, or for any right in subordinate officers to review his decision, and in effect defeat it. Whenever a statute gives a discretionary power to any person, to be exercised by him upon his own opinion of certain facts, it is a sound rule of construction that the statute constitutes him the sole and exclusive judge of the existence of these facts. . . . Such is the true construction of the act of 1795. It is no answer that such a power may be abused, for there is no power which is not susceptible of abuse. The remedy for this, as well as for all other misconduct, if it should occur, is to be found in the constitution itself. In a free government the danger must be remote, since in addition to the high qualities which the Executive must be presumed to possess, of public virtue and honest devotion to the public interests, *the frequency of elections, and the watchfulness of the representatives of the nation, carry with them all the checks which can be useful to guard against usurpation and wanton tyranny.*[4]

Taney for the Court in *Luther v. Borden* (1849):

After the President has acted and called out the militia, is a Circuit Court of the United States authorized to inquire

[4] This was an extremely important decision from the point of view of the federal system, for three New England governors in the War of 1812 had asserted that it was for them, not the President, to decide whether and when the militia was to be called out. For other cases constructive of the militia clause and laws, and of the President's powers thereunder, see *Houston v. Moore*, 5 Wheaton 1 (1820); *Presser v. Illinois*, 116 U.S. 252 (1886); *Johnson v. Sayre*, 158 U.S. 109, 115 (1895); *McLaughry v. Deming*, 186 U.S. 49 (1902); *Arver v. U.S.*, 245 U.S. 366, 381–387 (1918); *Cox v. Wood*, 247 U.S. 3, 5–6 (1918). The Court has been quick, as in the last of these cases, to repel the attempts of various citizens to shackle the war power with sophistries about the nature and purpose of the militia. Whether there are limits to the use of the militia is for the President to decide. See 29 *Opinions of the Attorney General* 322.

whether his decision was right? . . . If it could, then it would become the duty of the court (provided that it came to the conclusion that the President had decided incorrectly) to discharge those who were arrested or detained by the troops in the service of the United States. . . . *If the judicial power extends so far, the guarantee [of a republican form of government] contained in the Constitution of the United States is a guarantee of anarchy, and not of order.* Yet if this right does not reside in the courts when the conflict is raging, if the judicial power is at that time bound to follow the decision of the political, it must be equally bound when the contest is over.

It is said that this power in the President is dangerous to liberty, and may be abused. *All power may be abused if placed in unworthy hands. But it would be difficult, we think, to point out any other hands in which this power would be more safe, and at the same time equally effectual.* When citizens of the same State are in arms against each other, and the constituted authorities unable to execute the laws, the interposition of the United States must be prompt, or it is of little value. The ordinary course of proceedings in courts of justice would be utterly unfit for the crisis. *And the elevated office of the President, chosen as he is by the people of the United States, and the high responsibility he could not fail to feel when acting in a case of so much moment, appear to furnish as strong safeguards against a wilful abuse of power as human prudence and foresight could well provide. At all events, it is conferred upon him by the Constitution and laws of the United States, and must therefore be respected and enforced in its judicial tribunals.*

The common element in these opinions would seem to be a genuine judicial reluctance to speak in a situation where the voice of the Court, even if heard, could not have any effect. More than this, both Story and Taney seem to share the suspicion, unusual in them, that under a popular form of government there are certain questions that the political branches must be trusted to answer with finality.

It would be dangerous and misleading to push the principles of these cases too far, especially the doctrine of "political questions" as implied in *Luther v. Borden.* Given the opportunity to afford a grievously injured citizen relief from a palpably unwarranted use of presidential or military power, especially when the question at issue falls in the penumbra between the "political" and the "justiciable," the Court will act as if it had never heard of this doctrine and its underlying assumption that there are some powers against which the judiciary simply cannot be expected to act as the last line of defense. In the main, however—indeed, in 99 cases out of 100—the principle of *Martin v. Mott* and *Luther v. Borden,* expanded into a general rule for judicial review of presidential military action, will be faithfully applied. And that principle is this: When the President decides to use military force to preserve the peace, neither the decision itself nor the methods employed are open to question in the courts of the United States. In such instances, his discretion must control, and the courts cannot intervene and grant relief. Powerless in fact, they have chosen likewise to be powerless in law.[5]

[5] Two instructive cases of judicial scrutiny of a state governor's decisions in regard to martial law are *Moyer v. Peabody,* 212 U.S. 78 (1909), and *Sterling v. Constantin,* 287 U.S. 378 (1932).

Who Can Suspend the Writ of Habeas Corpus?

Ex parte Merryman

This is another of those constitutional posers that the framers, probably because they entertained no doubts and anticipated no troubles on the subject, left as an unanswered legacy to generations of lawyers, professors, and commentators. The Constitution grants this great emergency power to no one; it assumes its existence as a matter of fact and common law, and merely qualifies its employment in these terms: "The privilege of the writ of habeas corpus shall not be suspended, unless when in cases of rebellion and invasion the public safety may require it." No court has ever doubted that Congress could suspend the writ of habeas corpus in a condition of necessity. The point of controversy has been: Does the President, too, possess this power?

Constitutional theory answers *no*. The great commentators from Story to Willoughby,[6] relying on the location of the habeas corpus clause in the legislative article and supported by a dictum of Marshall in the early case *Ex*

[6] Joseph Story, *Commentaries on the Constitution* (Boston, 1833), secs. 1338–1342; W. W. Willoughby, *Constitutional Law of the United States* (New York, 1929), III, 1611–1615. See also J. N. Pomeroy, *An Introduction to the Constitutional Law of the United States* (7th ed.; Boston, 1883), 473–474; William Winthrop, *Military Law* (Washington, 1893), II, 54–56; J. R. Tucker, *The Constitution of the United States* (Chicago, 1899), II, 642–652; H. von Holst, *Constitutional Law of the United States* (Chicago, 1887), 196–197; C. K. Burdick, *The Law of the American Constitution* (New York, 1922), 84–85. This list is representative, not exclusive; there could be many additions.

18

parte Bollman,[7] have assumed with virtual unanimity that Congress alone possesses this authority. Historical fact, on the other hand, answers *yes.* In the one period in our history when the suspension of the writ became an overriding necessity, a President, Abraham Lincoln, suspended it on his own authority, not once but several times, without substantial interference from Court or Congress.[8]

Unfortunately for the purposes of this study, fact and theory have never clashed at the highest level. The Supreme Court has yet to speak directly on the constitutionality of presidential suspension. There is no doubt that the Court had several chances in the course of the rebellion to come to grips with this unsolved problem; but enough members of the Court were wary (and Attorney General Bates downright fearful) of a final trial of strength between executive and judiciary to prevent a conclusive decision.[9]

In the lower courts, however, this problem was directly at issue, and although some courts agreed with the opinion of Bates, several intrepid judges spoke out fearlessly in defiance of Lincoln's assumption of this spacious power.[10]

[7] 4 Cranch 75, 101 (1807).

[8] On Lincoln's suspension of the writ, see the admirable study of J. G. Randall, *Constitutional Problems under Lincoln* (New York, 1926), chaps. 6–8.

[9] Randall, *op. cit.,* 132.

[10] See the interesting opinions in *In re McDonald,* 16 Fed. Cas. 17 (1861), No. 8751; *Ex parte Benedict,* 3 Fed. Cas. 159 (1862), No. 1292; *Ex parte Field,* 9 Fed. Cas. 1 (1862), No. 4761; *McCall v. McDowell,* 16 Fed. Cas. 1235 (1867), No. 8673. As splendid examples of the critical attitude of some of the state courts, see *Jones v. Seward,* 40 Barb. (N.Y.) 563 (1863), and *In re Kemp,* 16 Wisc. 359 (1863). It was the adverse decision in the latter case that Bates advised Stanton to let go unappealed.

To the strictures of these lower-court judges Lincoln paid no heed, but on one opinion, we may feel sure, he dwelt with careful attention. Whatever his ideas in 1863 and 1864, he was not at all certain of his authority in the early months of the war, and an opinion of the Chief Justice denying that the President could ever suspend the writ of habeas corpus was certain to win a careful reading.

The case, of course, was *Ex parte Merryman*,[11] decided by Taney May 28, 1861, in the circuit court in Baltimore, not, as is commonly asserted, in the capacity of circuit justice, but as Chief Justice of the United States pure and simple, acting under section 14 of the Judiciary Act of 1789,[12] which provided that "either of the justices of the supreme court, as well as judges of the district courts, shall have power to grant writs of *habeas corpus* for the purpose of an inquiry into the cause of commitment." The circumstances of this case attracted a great deal of popular attention, and the elements of melodrama are in it even today. At no other time in all the long history of the Court have a President and a Chief Justice, or any justice for that matter, come into such direct conflict over an exercise of presidential power.

John Merryman, a leading citizen of the state of Maryland, had succeeded in making himself, through a variety of secessionist activities, a thorough nuisance to the military authorities trying to maintain order along the Philadelphia-Washington line of communications. Having

[11] 17 Fed. Cas. 144 (1861), No. 9487. For graphic accounts of this incident, see C. B. Swisher, *Roger B. Taney* (New York, 1935), 547–560; B. C. Steiner, *Roger Brooke Taney* (Baltimore, 1922), 490–504.

[12] 1 *Stat.* 72, 81.

been arrested and confined in Fort McHenry, one of the few places in seething Baltimore where the star-spangled banner yet waved, he petitioned for a writ of habeas corpus. Under ordinary circumstances he would have turned to the district court with his prayer, but a judge of that court had already been successfully defied by a major at Fort McHenry. It was plain that it would take a good deal more prestige than that of a district judge to tip the scales for justice in this unequal balance of the judicial and military powers. With the Supreme Court out of session, its members who remained in Washington were available to issue the writ, and who could have been more eager to do just that than the justice in whose circuit the court in Baltimore happened to fall? It is now an accepted fact that Taney, old and worn as he was, or perhaps because he was old and worn and had little to fear ("I was ever a fighter, so—one fight more, the best and the last!"), went from Washington to Baltimore for the specific purpose of entertaining Merryman's application. He did this, of course, in full knowledge of the President's order of April 27 authorizing the Commanding General of the United States Army or the proper officer to suspend the writ of habeas corpus "at any point or in the vicinity of any military line which is now or which shall be used between the city of Philadelphia and the city of Washington." [13]

The scenes of this drama unrolled at a pace that left the actors little time for reflection on the implications of their words and deeds. Merryman was carried off from his country estate at 2:00 A.M. on May 25, and petitioned for a writ of habeas corpus the very same day. On May 26

[13] J. D. Richardson, *Messages and Papers of the Presidents* (Washington, 1896–1899), VI, 18.

21

Taney issued the requested writ, directing General George Cadwalader to bring Merryman before him. At the appointed hour on May 27 the general's aide-de-camp, armed with his sword and girded in a bright red sash, appeared before the Chief Justice and politely but flatly refused to produce the prisoner, citing as authority the President's order of April 27. At the same time, he made clear the general's desire to postpone the action "until he can receive instructions from the President of the United States, when you shall hear further from him." Taney, who by now considered himself the last barricade between the Constitution and despotism, would have none of it, and ordered that an attachment for contempt be issued immediately against Cadwalader, returnable the following day.

The final scene was played on May 28. The Chief Justice, informed by the United States marshal that the guard at Fort McHenry had not permitted him to serve the attachment, excused him from any further action on the ground that "the power refusing obedience was so notoriously superior to any the marshal could command." To the several thousand people who had flocked to the courtroom half expecting to see Lincoln and Taney have it out face to face, he announced four points: that the President had no power under the Constitution to suspend the privilege of the writ of habeas corpus; that the military had no power, either of its own or by order of the President, to detain a civilian "except in aid of the judicial authority," which was clearly not the case in this affair; that Merryman was entitled to immediate discharge; and that he would file an opinion in writing within the week.

There is little that need be said about the content of this

opinion. A brief, straightforward exposition of the exclusive power of Congress to suspend the great writ, it relied heavily on Blackstone, Marshall, Jefferson, Story, and the location of the habeas corpus clause in the legislative article. The central proposition in Taney's argument, as in that of all those who deny this power to the executive, was as simple as this: "And if the high power over the liberty of the citizen now claimed, was intended to be conferred upon the president, it would undoubtedly be found in plain words in this article."

At the end of his opinion Taney pointed directly to the person who bore the responsibility for this action and who alone could correct it:

In such a case, my duty was too plain to be mistaken. I have exercised all the power which the constitution and laws confer upon me, but that power has been resisted by a force too strong for me to overcome. It is possible that the officer who has incurred this grave responsibility may have misunderstood his instructions, and exceeded the authority intended to be given him; I shall, therefore, order all the proceedings in this case, with my opinion, to be filed and recorded in the circuit court of the United States for the district of Maryland, and direct the clerk to transmit a copy, under seal, to the President of the United States. It will then remain for that high officer, in fulfillment of his constitutional obligation to take care that the laws be faithfully executed, to determine what measures he will take to cause the civil processes of the United States to be respected and enforced.

What Lincoln did with the copy sent to him, or what he thought of the entire incident, has never been disclosed. Taney returned to Washington unmolested; Lincoln went right on exercising the power that the Chief Justice had branded palpably unconstitutional; [14] and Merryman, after languishing a short time in Fort McHenry, was turned over to the civil authorities, indicted for treason, and eventually released. In his famous July 4 message to the special session of Congress Lincoln acknowledged that "the attention of the country has been called to the proposition that one who is sworn 'to take care that the laws be faithfully executed' should not himself violate them." He insisted that the question had been left open by the framers and that, in effect, the emergency of April, 1861, had answered it. In any case, he promised an "opinion at some length" from the Attorney General and left further action "entirely to the better judgment of Congress." On the following day Bates announced his opinion that the President shared with Congress the power to suspend the writ. [15]

Professor Swisher has written, "It is futile to argue whether the President or the Chief Justice was *right* in the matter, for back of their legal differences were fundamental differences of opinion on matters of public policy," and with this severely neutral judgment we can generally

[14] See particularly his sweeping suspension of the writ by proclamation of September 24, 1862, in Richardson, *op. cit.*, VI, 98–99. Lincoln plainly regarded the Act of 1863 (12 *Stat.* 755), authorizing him to suspend the writ, merely as declaratory.

[15] Richardson, *op. cit.*, VI, 20–31, especially 24–25. The opinion of Bates is in 10 *O.A.G.* 74–85, especially 81–85. Lincoln's chief unofficial support came from the distinguished lawyer Horace Binney. See his *The Privilege of the Writ of Habeas Corpus* (Philadelphia, 1862), and other works. In criticism of this stand, see S. G. Fisher, "The Suspension of Habeas Corpus during the War of the Rebellion," *Political Science Quarterly*, III (1888), 454–488; there is an invaluable bibliography at 485–488. The mixed attitude of Congress is depicted in G. C. Sellery, *Lincoln's Suspension of Habeas Corpus as Viewed by Congress* (Madison, Wisc., 1907).

agree.[16] Taney was a judge, Lincoln an executive. Taney was from Maryland and had delivered the opinion in *Scott v. Sanford;* Lincoln was from Illinois and had ridiculed that holding. It certainly cannot be said that Taney had one shred more respect than Lincoln for the rights of his fellow citizens, especially the rights of those who disagreed with him. Indeed, we know that the contrary was true. In the end, it was simply a question of this: Taney as Chief Justice was anxious to preserve respect for the law; Lincoln as President was determined to preserve the Union.

It would seem equally futile to argue over the present location of this power, for it is a question on which fact and theory cannot be expected to concur. Today, as ninety years ago, the answer to it is not to be found in law but in circumstance. The one great precedent is what Lincoln did, not what Taney said. Future Presidents will know where to look for historical support. So long as public opinion sustains the President, as a sufficient amount of it sustained Lincoln in his shadowy tilt with Taney and throughout the rest of the war, he has nothing to fear from the displeasure of the courts. If he should misread the necessity and find public opinion overwhelmingly against him, he can always, like Jackson at New Orleans, submit to the court with a speech to the gallery and turn the incident into a personal triumph! The law of the Constitution, as it actually exists, must be considered to read that in a condition of martial necessity the President has the power to suspend the privilege of the writ of habeas corpus. The most a court or judge can do is read the President a lecture based on *Ex parte Merryman.* And the chief

[16] Swisher, *Taney*, 555.

end that such a lecture will doubtless serve—it was certainly true of Taney's opinion—will be that of a handy weapon for agitators, obstructionists, and haters of "that man in the White House."

The Great Exception:
Ex parte Milligan

Of all the arbitrary executive practices in which Lincoln found it imperative to engage, certainly the most dubious and judicially assailable was the trial of civilians by military commission. It was one thing for him to proclaim a blockade of the South, suspend the writ of habeas corpus along the nation's most important line of communications, raise the limits of the regular forces in the absence of Congress, or even issue the Emancipation Proclamation while denying that Congress had any such power. It was quite another, certainly in a country that could trace its legal history back through the Petition of Right, to authorize military trial of disaffected civilians in areas where the civil courts were open and functioning. Yet this is precisely what Lincoln did in his proclamation of September 24, 1862. The importance of this document demands that it be quoted in full:

Whereas it has become necessary to call into service not only volunteers, but also portions of the militia of the States by draft in order to suppress the insurrection existing in the United States, and disloyal persons are not adequately restrained by the ordinary processes of law from hindering this measure and from giving aid and comfort in various ways to the insurrection:

Now, therefore, be it ordered, first, that during the existing insurrection, and as a necessary measure for suppressing the same, all rebels and insurgents, their aiders and abettors, within the United States, and all persons discouraging volunteer enlistments, resisting militia drafts, or guilty of any disloyal practice affording aid and comfort to rebels against the authority of the United States, shall be subject to martial law and liable to trial and punishment by courts-martial or military commissions; second, that the writ of *habeas corpus* is suspended in respect to all persons arrested, or who are now or hereafter during the rebellion shall be imprisoned in any fort, camp, arsenal, military prison, or other place of confinement by any military authority or by the sentence of any court-martial or military commission.[17]

One year later, September 15, 1863, he issued a second proclamation suspending the privilege of such persons to the great writ, and this time cited as authority the Habeas Corpus Act of 1863.[18] He did not mention the subject of military commissions, and it is extremely important to note that Congress did not authorize them in this act. Whatever military trials of civilians took place during the war found their authority in the President's position as commander in chief.

Here, it will be said, was the point at which the courts of the United States, led by an indignant Supreme Court, called a halt to the President's cavalier treatment of the Constitution. Certainly the constitutional guarantee of jury trial and the procedural rights outlined in Amendments IV, V, and VI prevented trial by military commission in areas where the regular courts were open, whatever might have become of these rights in Kentucky or

---

[17] Richardson, *op. cit.*, VI, 98–99; 13 *Stat.* 730.
[18] *Ibid.*, 170–171; 13 *Stat.* 734.

Tennessee or reconquered Louisiana. Certainly they did, and yet there is no case on the records of the Supreme Court or other federal courts in which this practice was impugned in the course of the war; first, because trials of this nature in areas where the regular courts were functioning were extremely rare, since the normal method of dealing with persons suspected of treasonable activity was arrest without warrant, detention without trial, and release without punishment; second, because most federal courts went out of their way to avoid a brush with the military authorities; and, third, because the Supreme Court itself put a damper on attempts to challenge the constitutionality of these controversial trials by military commission through an interesting decision announced in February, 1864.

The case in question, *Ex parte Vallandigham*,[19] involved the petition of the notorious Peace Democrat Clement L. Vallandigham "for a *certiorari*, to be directed to the Judge Advocate General of the Army of the United States, to send up [to the Supreme Court] for its review, the proceedings of a military commission" by which he had been tried in Cincinnati in May, 1863 (on a charge of publicly expressing sympathy for the enemy), and had been sentenced to prison for the duration. A few days after the trial the President commuted this sentence to banishment to rebel territory. Vallandigham, who apparently didn't think much of the celebrated query, "If he doesn't like it here, why doesn't he go back where he came from?" made a grand circuit through Bermuda and Halifax, and within six weeks was settled down across the river from Detroit. From this vantage point he ran for Governor of Ohio on

[19] 1 Wallace 243 (1864).

28

the Democratic ticket and watched his case pushed through to the Supreme Court.[20]

The Court refused to touch it. Seizing with evident relief upon the circumstance that the district court in Cincinnati had refused to issue a writ of habeas corpus to General Burnside and had thus forced Vallandigham to take his case directly from military commission to Supreme Court, the judges beat a unanimous retreat to the fortress of technicality. They declined to accept the case, on the ground that the military commission was not a "court" within the meaning of the Constitution or the section of the Judiciary Act of 1789 that granted the Court its appellate jurisdiction.[21] Moreover, the doctrine of *Marbury v. Madison* concerning the sharply defined limits of the Court's original jurisdiction forebade it to issue a writ of habeas corpus to the military authorities. Thus was staved off a potentially explosive judgment on the validity of the arrests and military trials ordered by Lincoln and Stanton.

The only indication of the Court's attitude on this great question was a cryptic remark at the close of Wayne's opinion: "And as to the President's action in such matters, and those acting in them under his authority, we refer to the opinions expressed by this court, in the cases of *Martin v. Mott*, and *Dynes v. Hoover*." In each of these opinions, the latter of which Wayne had delivered,[22] the Court sup-

[20] In June, 1864, he slipped back into Ohio and spent the rest of the war agitating, while Lincoln looked the other way. Carl Sandburg, *Abraham Lincoln: The War Years* (New York, 1939), III, 109.

[21] 1 *Stat.* 73, 81.

[22] 20 Howard 65 (1857). The case involved a challenge on technical grounds to the jurisdiction and sentence of a Navy court-martial.

ported strongly the jurisdiction and sentence of a court-martial. In the first was expressed, in the second implied, an equally strong opinion that the President in acting under his military powers should be accorded great if not conclusive discretion. Since the three justices (Nelson, Grier, and Field) who concurred in the decision of *Ex parte Vallandigham* but not in the opinion were with the extreme limitationists in the next case of this type to come before the Court, it seems safe to assume that with this remark Wayne went out of his way to make clear that no censure of the President was to be implied from this decision. This, however, is circumstantial conjecture. As a final observation on this case, Wayne's opinion was based squarely on the reasoning of Judge Advocate General Holt, just as squarely as an opinion could be on argument of counsel at the bar.

Nothing more concerning the legality of military commissions was heard in the courts of the United States until the end of the war. Then, on April 3, 1866, some 353 days after Lincoln's assassination, a Supreme Court that included five of his appointments announced its unanimous conviction that the President had acted unconstitutionally in instituting trial by military commission during the war in areas where the civil courts were open and functioning. Five of the judges (Davis, Nelson, Grier, Clifford, and Field) went further and denied this power to Congress as well; the other four (Chase, Wayne, Swayne, and Miller) refused to join in this far-reaching dictum. At first, the decision went virtually unnoticed, for the opinions were not delivered until December 17, 1866, nor made public until two weeks later. Then, however, the country erupted into the most violent and partisan agitation over a

Supreme Court decision since the days of Dred Scott. The views of the majority on the lack of power in Congress to institute military tribunals, which were not necessary to the decision and could only be regarded as a gratuitous salvo against the plans of the Radicals for congressional reconstruction, split the nation, or at least its press, into two hotheaded camps.[23] Mr. Lincoln and his commissions were all but forgotten in the exultation of the Democrats and recriminations of the Radicals.

Today, of course, we remember this case for its construction of the President's war powers as well as for its celebrated defense of the inviolability of the Constitution in time of crisis. It is from this point of view that we should set out the facts and evaluate the opinions in *Ex parte Milligan.*

Lambdin P. Milligan, a "Son of Liberty" who had done a great deal more than merely give speeches in defiance of Lincoln and the Union, was arrested October 5, 1864, at his home in Indiana, tried by a military commission established under presidential authority, and sentenced to be hanged May 9, 1865, for disloyal activities. This sentence was approved by President Johnson. At the time of his arrest and trial the circuit court in Indianapolis was open for business and fully prepared to take cognizance of his case under the procedures outlined in the Habeas Corpus Act of 1863. Sections 2 and 3 of this law provided in sub-

[23] See the magnificent account of this affair in Charles Warren, *The Supreme Court in United States History* (New York, 1926), II, 423–449. To me this is easily the most fascinating part of a great, if unbalanced and uncritical, book, even though I cannot agree that *Ex parte Milligan* "has since been recognized by all men as the palladium of the rights of the individual." See also Samuel Klaus, *The Milligan Case* (New York, 1929).

31

stance that lists of prisoners arrested under authority of the President were to be furnished by the Secretaries of State and War to the circuit- and district-court judges. If grand juries returned no indictments against them, they were to be discharged by judicial order upon taking an oath of allegiance and entering into recognizance for good behavior. Where such lists were not furnished, a judge could discharge a prisoner on a writ of habeas corpus if satisfied of his loyalty. This process had been completely ignored in Milligan's case.

On May 10, 1865, with the noose practically around his neck, Milligan sued out a writ of habeas corpus to the circuit court in Indianapolis, and on a division of opinion the case was brought before the Supreme Court. The linchpin that had been missing in *Ex parte Vallandigham* was supplied by a circuit court able and willing to be heard in military circles. The arguments in this case, which took place in March, 1866, pitted the illustrious team of Attorney General Speed, Attorney General-to-be Stanbery, and General Benjamin F. Butler against the still more illustrious team of David Dudley Field, James A. Garfield, and Jeremiah S. Black. Lest it be thought that these gentlemen were arguing over the disposition of a corpse, it should be remarked that Milligan was very much alive. His sentence of hanging had been stayed on May 10 and had later been commuted to life imprisonment by President Johnson. Apparently no one had bothered to inform the Court, for at one point Davis paused to remark, "Although we have no judicial information on the subject, yet the inference is that he is still alive; for otherwise learned counsel would not appear for him and urge this court to decide his case."

It is impossible to express in capsule form the right-eousness, one might say self-righteousness, of Davis' opinion for the Court. He, like Taney, elected to turn a fairly simple case into a defense of "the very framework of the government and the fundamental principles of American liberty," with the obvious difference that Taney had been in the trenches, while Davis was well to the rear. In any case, he made the specific points that this presi-dentially authorized military commission had no juris-diction to try and sentence Milligan, that the writ of habeas corpus ought immediately to issue, and that the prisoner should thereupon be discharged from custody. His general holding has already been mentioned: The President has no power under the Constitution to institute a military commission for trial of civilians in areas where the regular courts are open for business. It was his further observations that an invasion of American soil had actually to be under way, not merely threatened, to permit a state of martial law, and that Congress itself could not have authorized these commissions, which drew the fire of four of the justices. "We think," said Chase, thinking of his friends in Congress and the election of 1868, "that Con-gress had power, though not exercised, to authorize the military commission which was held in Indiana." All nine agreed, however, that Lincoln, whose name was never mentioned in argument or opinion but with reverence and awe, had gone well beyond the limits of his authority as commander in chief to maintain order among the civilian population. Finally, although both Davis and the Chief Justice had a great deal to say about the writ of habeas corpus, neither attempted to decide the question upon which Lincoln and Taney had clashed.

33

There remain to be quoted the most famous lines of Davis' opinion:

The Constitution of the United States is a law for rulers and people, equally in war and in peace, and covers with the shield of its protection all classes of men, at all times, and under all circumstances. No doctrine involving more pernicious consequences was ever invented by the wit of man than that any of its provisions can be suspended during any of the great exigencies of government. Such a doctrine leads directly to anarchy or despotism, but the theory of necessity on which it is based is false; for the government, within the Constitution, has all the powers granted to it which are necessary to preserve its existence; as has been happily proved by the result of the great effort to throw off its just authority.[24]

A great deal of praise and condemnation has been heaped indiscriminately upon *Ex parte Milligan*. For that reason, it is necessary to stand back a little from this case, look once again at its history and opinions in the light of facts and not legends, and attempt to appraise its true value as a restraint upon and interpretation of the exercise of the President's power as commander in chief.

As a restrain upon a President beset by martial crisis it was then, and is now, of practically no value whatsoever. It cannot be emphasized too strongly that the decision in this case followed the close of the rebellion by a full year, altered not in the slightest degree the extraordinary methods through which that rebellion had been suppressed, and did nothing more than deliver from jail a handful of rascals who in any event would have probably gained their freedom in short order. For Johnson it was, if anything, an extra round of ammunition to be fired at

[24] 4 Wallace 2, 120–121.

34

Thad Stevens. And upon all Presidents who have come after, it has had precious little demonstrable effect. True, it has been urged upon the Court many times in the hope of restraining some unusual presidential or congressional action, but never yet has it gained an important victory. No justice has ever altered his opinion in a case of liberty against authority because counsel for liberty recited *Ex parte Milligan*. Judges, too, are practical men, and when they decide for liberty, as happily they often do, they do it for better reasons than the fact that once upon a time a Supreme Court scolded a President who had saved the Union and had been shot for his pains, especially since that same Court with but one change in personnel had failed to scold him earlier when it might have done some good.

It is often argued that, quite apart from the practical influence this case has had or could have as a weapon for Court, Congress, and people to use in keeping a crisis-minded President in line, the moral value of Davis' opinion as a lecture to all future Presidents must assign it a place high on the list of the great cases. But this is to ignore the fact that no President, certainly not Cleveland or Wilson or the two Roosevelts, seems to have given it the slightest thought in determining the scope and form of his martial powers, and that in any case Davis so overstated his point as to render his observations wholly meaningless for a constitutional government determined to stay alive in a strife-torn world. The Constitution of the United States does *not* cover "with the shield of its protection all classes of men, at all times and under all circumstances," and there is nothing to be gained by insisting that it does. Would that it did—or, better, would that it could.

35

As an interpretation of presidential power the Milligan case has considerably more standing. It was important, even at that late date, to announce that there were, after all, some limits to the President's power over the civilian population well behind the lines. The use of military commissions in Indiana in 1864 was, it must be agreed, plainly unconstitutional, and even Lincoln's defenders could wish that he had shunned this extraordinary practice. It is no answer to point out that the regular courts, principally by reason of the jury system, were more hindrance than help to the cause of the Union; for if the military authorities did not trust the civil courts, they had only to keep their suspects locked up until the danger had passed. This, indeed, was the usual method of handling these cases. In other words, it was arguable that, under the conditions then obtaining, Milligan should be denied the privilege of the writ, but it was not necessary to go further and place him on trial before a military court. To this extent, Davis' opinion rested on solid ground.

But on several other points it flew far too high and wide. It is simply not true that "martial law cannot arise from a *threatened* invasion," or that "martial rule can never exist where the courts are open." These statements do not present an accurate definition of the allowable limits of the martial powers of President and Congress in the face of alien threats or internal disorder. Nor was Davis' dictum on the specific power of Congress in this matter any more accurate. And, however eloquent and quotable his words on the untouchability of the Constitution in time of actual crisis, they do not now, and did not then, express the realities of American constitutional law.

Finally, viewed simply as a conspicuous link in the long

36

chain of decisions on liberty and authority that stretch from 1 *Dallas* to the present, *Ex parte Milligan* was an exhibition of judicial self-hypnosis of which no clearheaded friend of the Court could possibly be proud. It is not easy for the layman to see the alleged decisive difference between *Ex parte Vallandigham* and *Ex parte Milligan.* The decision in the former has a hollow ring, which makes the echo of the latter even more hollow. If the Court had been at all anxious to test the President's reading of his powers —if, for example, Davis had really believed that the Constitution meant what it said about trial by jury—it would have been no trouble at all to alter Vallandigham's petition from one for certiorari to one for a writ of habeas corpus, returnable before one of the justices, if not the Court itself.[25] The Court could certainly have done what another Court was later to do in *Ex parte Grossman:* [26] entertain as an original suit the petition for a writ of habeas corpus of an individual unable to get justice from a recalcitrant (or spineless) lower federal court.

The answer, of course, is that Vallandigham got the ear of the Court in February, 1864, Milligan in March, 1866. Davis himself, at the outset of his opinion, betrayed this crucial point in these remarkable words:

During the late wicked Rebellion, the temper of the times did not allow that calmness in deliberation and discussion so necessary to a correct conclusion of a purely judicial [sic!] question. *Then,* considerations of safety were mingled with the exercise of power; and feelings and interests prevailed which are happily terminated. *Now* that the public safety is

[25] See 2 Wallace 243, 252 for the Court's shaky explanation of its inability to do this.

[26] 267 U.S. 87 (1925).

assured, this question, as well as all others, can be discussed and decided without passion or the admixture of any element not required to form a legal judgment. We approach the investigation of this case, fully sensible of the magnitude of the inquiry and the necessity of full and cautious deliberation.[27]

And, he might have added, entirely free to decide against the executive power without inviting the accusation that the Court was obstructing the President's efforts to lay the rebellion. It is one thing for a Court to lecture a President when the emergency has passed, quite another to stand up in the middle of the battle and inform him that he is behaving unconstitutionally. There is no intention here to deride the Court for executing its retreat of 1864. At that time discretion was indeed the better part of valor, and the Court practically confessed the futility of judicial restraint on a President actively exercising his war powers in defense of an embattled nation. There is, however, a clear intention, openly avowed and resolutely pursued, to blast that "evident piece of arrant hypocrisy," [28] *Ex parte Milligan.* Perhaps this assessment has been too hard on Davis and his brethren. He was a good and patriotic man, and so were most of his associates. He was a confused man, too, for on one hand he had been a great friend of Lincoln, and on the other he was deeply concerned over the spirit of disrespect for the Constitution that the war had touched off and that reconstruction was fanning ever higher. His anxieties, and his muddleheadedness, too, are plain in this passage:

This nation, as experience has proved, cannot always remain at peace, and has no right to expect that it will always

[27] 2 Wallace 109. The italics are his, not mine.
[28] E. S. Corwin, *The President* (2d ed.; New York, 1941), 165.

38

have wise and humane rulers, sincerely attached to the principles of the Constitution. Wicked men, ambitious of power, with hatred of liberty and contempt of law, may fill the place once occupied by Washington and Lincoln; and if this right is conceded, and the calamities of war again befall us, the dangers to human liberty are frightful to contemplate.[29]

He was doing his sincere best to preserve our constitutional future, but even here he tripped over his own ambivalence, for the one thing upon which all nine justices were agreed was that Lincoln had *not* been "sincerely attached to the principles of the Constitution." If this Court had not been willing or able to restrain that "wise and humane ruler," how could any future Court, even if armed with *Ex parte Milligan,* be expected to check a "wicked man, ambitious of power, with hatred of liberty and contempt of law"? In effect, he was rejecting the sound advice of Story in *Martin v. Mott* and Taney in *Luther v. Borden* that the character and devotion to duty of the President himself must ever be the principal checks on the abuse of executive power.

In sum, *Ex parte Milligan* is sound doctrine in forbidding the presidential establishment of military commissions for the trial of civilians in areas where the civil courts are open—but it is little else. Its general observations on the limits of the war powers are no more valid today than they were in 1866. Here again the law of the Constitution is what Lincoln did in the crisis, not what the Court said later.[30]

[29] 2 Wallace 125.

[30] One other Civil War case, which will be treated at length below (pp. 68–77), should be mentioned here. In the *Prize Cases,* 2 Black 635, 671–674 (1863), the majority held, in effect, that the President could brand and treat as enemies of the United States

SUPREME COURT AND COMMANDER IN CHIEF

Martial Rule in World War II:
The Case of the Japanese-Americans

From *Ex parte Milligan* to the second year of World War II only one major case concerning the President's power of martial rule came to the Court for decision. In *In re Debs* a unanimous Court gave its unqualified blessing to the President's authority, even in defiance of the wishes of a state governor, to call out the troops in defense of the nation's interests, property, and powers.

"We hold it to be an incontrovertible principle, that the government of the United States may, by means of physical force, exercised through its official agents, execute on every foot of American soil the powers and functions that belong to it. This necessarily involves the power to command obedience to its laws, and hence the power to keep the peace to that extent."

The entire strength of the nation may be used to enforce in any part of the land the full and free exercise of all national powers and the security of all rights entrusted by the Constitution to its care. The strong arm of the national government may be put forth to brush away all obstructions to the freedom of interstate commerce or the transportation of the mails. If the emergency arises, the army of the Nation, and all its militia, are at the service of the nation to compel obedience to its laws.[31]

all inhabitants of an area in general insurrection against the federal government. This pushes his power of martial rule to fantastic extremes. See also *Ford v. Surget*, 97 U.S. 594, 604 (1878).

[31] 158 U.S. 564, 578–579, 582 (1895). The first paragraph was a quote from Bradley's opinion in *Ex parte Siebold*, 100 U.S. 371, 395 (1879), in which he was discussing the power of United States marshals to perform certain duties in connection with elections.

40

The strong bias of the justices in favor of corporate property and against Governor Altgeld led them farther down the road to the Jackson-Lincoln-Roosevelt theory of the Presidency than the Court is usually inclined to go. Yet Brewer painted a remarkably accurate likeness of the President's actual powers to protect the peace. The Court had already made clear, in the memorable case *In re Neagle,*[32] that the "peace of the United States" would require a good deal of protection. In the light of the Debs and Neagle cases, it might easily be argued that there are no judicial limits to the President's real or alleged "inherent" power to protect the peace of the United States.

Otherwise these seventy-five years were barren of judicial discussion of this momentous problem. The Spanish-American War certainly raised no controversies of any basic importance over presidential or congressional war powers, and even World War I came and went without presenting the Court a single opportunity to lecture the President on such matters as habeas corpus, military commissions, martial law, and the use of troops. Wilson, recognizing the profound differences in character between his war and Lincoln's, made it clear from the outset that he was opposed to military trial of sedition and espionage cases as unconstitutional and as bad policy. Although numbers of Americans of questionable loyalty were roughly handled in the course of the war, in each instance it was at the hands of a civil court and a jury of fellow citizens acting under the broadly permissive terms of the Espionage Act of 1917, the "Sedition Law" amendment of 1918, and provisions in several other acts. In *Schenck v. United States* and *Abrams v. United States* the power of

[32] 135 U.S. 1, 58–68 (1890).

Congress to pass these laws, and of the Department of Justice to enforce them, was strongly, perhaps a little too strongly, upheld.[33]

World War II, however, was a different matter, for it brought in its wake three unusual exercises of military power over civilians, all grounded on the President's authority as commander in chief: the evacuation of the west coast Japanese-Americans, the declaration and maintenance of martial law in Hawaii, and the sixty-odd seizures of plants and industries in which labor disputes were injuring the war effort. Each of these programs was attacked in the courts by persons who had received arbitrary treatment at the hands of the military.

The evacuation of the Japanese-Americans is by now so familiar a tale that it will be retold here only so far as necessary to establish its significance for the President's power of martial rule, the ability of the Court to restrain that power, and the present standing of *Ex parte Milligan*.[34] The facts in brief are these: On February 19, 1942, in response to an overwhelming combination of military, journalistic, and congressional pressures, President Roosevelt issued Executive Order 9066,[35] which endowed the Secretary of War "and the Military Commanders whom he may from time to time designate" with broad discretionary authority to establish "military areas" from which

[33] 40 *Stat.* 76, 217, 411, 553. 249 U.S. 47 (1919); 249 U.S. 211 (1919); 250 U.S. 616 (1919).

[34] See generally the books and articles cited in Rossiter, *Constitutional Dictatorship*, 280–282; the first-rate study of Morton Grodzins, *Americans Betrayed* (Chicago, 1949); the legal literature cited by Grodzins at 351, especially the articles of Dembitz, Fairman, Rostow, and Freeman; and Leonard Bloom and Ruth Riemer, *Removal and Return* (Berkeley, Cal., 1949).

[35] 7 *Federal Register* 1407.

"any or all persons" might be excluded in order to prevent espionage and sabotage. The Secretary was directed to provide food, shelter, and transportation for such persons as were to be evacuated from a military area, and "the use of Federal Troops" to assist in enforcing compliance with his orders was authorized. All this was done "by virtue of the authority vested in me as President of the United States, and Commander in Chief of the Army and Navy." Although the order spoke in general terms that permitted the Secretary of War the fullest discretion to use this grant of power anywhere in the United States, it was a notorious fact that the Japanese-American population of the Pacific states was the target in mind. In all this Mr. Roosevelt acted in good faith, relying, as perforce he had to rely, on the opinions and advice of his civil and military subordinates.

The following day Secretary of War Henry L. Stimson delegated this authority to Lieutenant General J. L. DeWitt, commanding the so-called Western Defense Command. General DeWitt in his turn established by proclamation "Military Areas Nos. 1 and 2," consisting of the three westernmost states and part of Arizona. By a series of 108 separate orders he then, with the aid of the troops under his command and the War Relocation Authority (established by another executive order on March 18, 1942),[36] proceeded to remove all persons of Japanese ancestry from these two areas. This process was not finally completed, be it noted, until October, 1942. Both the coastal and eastern portions of the designated states were in this manner cleared of some 112,000 persons who answered the racial criterion established by DeWitt's orders.

[36] 7 *Fed. Reg.* 2165.

Fully 70,000 of this number were full-fledged citizens of the United States, by every legal, constitutional, and moral standard enjoying all the rights and privileges of all other citizens of the United States. Yet New Year's Day, 1943, found them locked up in a chain of camps in the interior hundreds and even thousands of miles from their homes. Many of the homes had already been occupied by fellow citizens fortunate enough to lack Japanese blood. The official explanation for this enforced mass evacuation was that it was a "military necessity." In the event of a Japanese assault on the Pacific coast, said the Army, the presence of thousands of disloyal or unpredictable people of Japanese descent might easily prove an element of confusion that the enemy could exploit to excessive advantage. Nor was there time for individual examination to separate the loyal from the disloyal.

Lest it be assumed that Congress looked askance at this extraordinary move by the President, it should be recorded that on March 21, 1942, by a voice vote, the two houses passed a law that substantially ratified and confirmed Executive Order 9066 by making a federal misdemeanor (punishable by a $5000 fine, a year in jail, or both) of any action in violation of the restrictions and orders laid down by the President, Secretary of War, and military commanders.[37] This eleven-line statute became law on March 21.

The judicial history of the Japanese-American evacuation consists primarily of three leading cases: *Hirabayashi v. United States*, decided June 21, 1943; [38] *Korematsu v.*

[37] 56 *Stat.* 173; 88 *Congressional Record* 2722–2726, 2729–2730.
[38] 320 U.S. 81 (1943). See 46 Fed. Supp. 657 (1942). See also *Yasui v. U.S.*, 320 U.S. 115 (1943).

United States, decided December 18, 1944;[39] and *Ex parte Endo,* decided the same day.[40] Even the dates of these cases give pause for sober reflection.

Hirabayashi v. United States. Gordon Hirabayashi, an American citizen and a senior at the University of Washington, was tried and convicted in the district court for violating two orders issued by General DeWitt: one directing him to report at a certain time to a "civil control station" (a preliminary to evacuation), the second a curfew regulation. He was sentenced under the Act of March 21, 1942, to imprisonment for three months on each count, the sentences to run concurrently. The circuit court heard his appeal and certified questions of law to the Supreme Court, whereupon the latter ordered the entire record brought before it.

The Court was in a position to follow either of two paths, one short and smooth, the other rocky and full of traps. It could review Hirabayashi's conviction on both counts, in which case it would have to examine the legality of the order commanding him to report to the control station, and thus might be forced into considering the constitutionality of the entire program of evacuation. Or it could confine itself to one count, and, if it found him guilty, could then ignore the other count, since the two sentences ran concurrently.[41] The Court selected the second path, fixing its attention rigidly on the much narrower issue of the curfew violation.

A unanimous Court found the general's order valid and sustained the conviction. Chief Justice Stone had little

[39] 323 U.S. 214 (1944); 140 Fed. 2d 289 (1943). Rehearing denied February 12, 1945; 324 U.S. 885.

[40] 323 U.S. 283 (1944).

[41] On this point, see *Brooks v. U.S.,* 267 U.S. 432, 441 (1925).

trouble repelling the two principal attacks on the curfew order. To the contention that the Act of March 21 was an unconstitutional delegation of legislative power, he retorted with the well-worn formulas and citations of the *Brig Aurora* and *Opp Cotton Mills v. Administrator.*[42] To the more serious contention that a curfew regulation discriminating between "citizens of Japanese ancestry and those of other ancestries" violated the Fifth Amendment, he replied that "the actions taken must be appraised in the light of the conditions with which the President and Congress were confronted in the early months of 1942." A nine-page review of these conditions—the Japanese victories, the exposed condition of the west coast, the unusual number of defense plants in that area, the peculiar problem of the Japanese-American population—led the Chief Justice to this conclusion:

We cannot close our eyes to the fact, demonstrated by experience, that in time of war residents having ethnic affiliations with an invading enemy may be a greater source of danger than those of different ancestry. Nor can we deny that Congress, and the military authorities acting with its authorization, have constitutional power to appraise the danger in the light of facts of public notoriety. We need not now attempt to define the ultimate boundaries of the war power. We decide only the issue as we have defined it—we decide only that the curfew order as applied, and at the time it was applied, was within the boundaries of the war power. In this case it is enough that circumstances within the knowledge of those charged with the responsibility for maintaining the national defense afforded a rational basis for the decision which they made. Whether we would have made it is irrelevant.

[42] 7 Cranch 382 (1812); 312 U.S. 126 (1941).

46

Hirabayashi v. United States is perhaps the most clear-cut case on record of the Court's tendency to insist that unusual military actions be grounded, whenever possible, on the combined powers of President and Congress, which when merged are called simply "the war powers of the United States." In this instance, thanks to the Act of March 21, the Court could state, "We have no occasion to consider whether the President, acting alone, could lawfully have made the curfew order in question or have authorized others to make it." With the aid of this formula, and confining itself strictly to the simple problem of a fairly reasonable curfew regulation, the Court had no trouble sustaining the government. Justices Douglas, Murphy, and Rutledge, in concurring with the result, warned that there were limits to this sort of thing. "In my opinion," said Murphy, "this goes to the very brink of constitutional power."

Ex parte Endo. Not until eighteen months later did the Court again find it necessary to think publicly about the Japanese-Americans, when two cases came before it for decision. The plea of Mitsuye Endo, an American citizen of demonstrated loyalty (she was a permanent employee in the California Civil Service), was simple and easily satisfied. She was evacuated in 1942 from Sacramento to a relocation center near Tule Lake, California, from which place she petitioned the district court unsuccessfully for discharge on a writ of habeas corpus. (Her petition was filed in July, 1942, and denied in July, 1943.) On appeal to the circuit court and certificate of questions of law to the Supreme Court (April 22, 1944), the entire record was passed up for final scrutiny. In the meantime Miss Endo had been removed to a camp in Utah, from which

47

she could gain release only under a series of conditions designed to prevent "a dangerously disorderly migration of unwanted people to unprepared communities." By the date of the decision the military areas had been disestablished and the relocation centers were being broken up. Under the circumstances the Court had no trouble in sidestepping the great constitutional issues—for which it was castigated by Justice Roberts in a separate opinion—and in holding that Miss Endo had been entitled all along to an unconditional release by the War Relocation Authority. In other words, even if evacuation of a loyal person from California had been warranted, detention in Utah had not been—definitely not by statute or order, probably not by the Constitution. The fact that she had been detained for several years and was already free to go her way in peace was not mentioned.

Korematsu v. United States. It was in the case of this citizen, convicted in the district court for remaining in his home in San Leandro, California, contrary to an exclusion order of General DeWitt,[43] that the Court was finally brought to an unavoidable consideration of the great constitutional questions raised by the evacuation. In a 6–3 decision, with Justice Black speaking for the majority and Justices Murphy, Roberts, and Jackson filing separate dissents, the Court upheld the program, and thus the exclusion order, as a valid exercise of presidential-military-congressional power, "as of the time it was made and when the petitioner violated it," and rejected the

[43] The general had the Japanese-Americans "coming and going." One order forbade them to leave the area, another to remain in it! The result, fully intended, was to force them to report to the evacuation stations. This is what Korematsu would not do. In effect, he was punished for sitting in his own home.

48

charges of counsel for Korematsu that it violated Amendments IV, V, VI, VII, and VIII.

Black's brief opinion was based on these very simple propositions: "There was evidence of disloyalty on the part of some, the military authorities considered that the need for action was great, and time was short. We cannot —by availing ourselves of the calm perspective of hindsight—now say that at that time these actions were unjustified." He denied that the evacuation was founded in racial prejudice, pointing out that the authorities had made their decision on the purely military basis of security against invasion, espionage, and sabotage. And to the Japanese-Americans he said:

We are not unmindful of the hardships imposed . . . upon a large group of American citizens. But hardships are part of war, and war is an aggregation of hardships. All citizens alike, both in and out of uniform, feel the impact of war in greater or lesser measure. Citizenship has its responsibilities as well as its privileges, and in time of war the burden is always heavier. Compulsory exclusion of large groups of citizens from their homes, except under circumstances of direct emergency and peril, is inconsistent with our basic governmental institutions. But when under conditions of modern warfare our shores are threatened by hostile forces, the power to protect must be commensurate with the threatened danger.

Since the Court had decided that it was constrained to accept the military's judgment of the extent of this danger, it was likewise constrained to accept its judgment of the extent of "the power to protect."

Justice Roberts dissented in a biting opinion. "This is not a case of keeping people off the streets at night as was *Hirabayashi v. U.S.* . . . On the contrary, it is the case of convicting a citizen as a punishment for not submitting to imprisonment in a concentration camp based on his ancestry, and solely because of his ancestry, without evidence or inquiry concerning his loyalty or good disposition towards the United States." He would not go so far as to hold that an evacuation of this sort would never be justified, but declared that "no pronouncement of the commanding officer can . . . preclude judicial inquiry and determine" whether a sufficient emergency had in fact existed. In this instance, he was certain, it had not.

Justice Murphy's words bit even deeper. "This exclusion . . . goes over 'the very brink of constitutional power' and falls into the ugly abyss of racism." He had apparently bothered to read the military and congressional reports on the evacuation, and had been shocked by the evidences of naked prejudice that ran like angry veins of poison through its entire history. Admitting frankly that the judgments of the military "ought not to be overruled lightly by those whose training and duties ill-equip them to deal intelligently with matters so vital to the physical security of the nation," he nevertheless felt that such a judgment "based upon such racial and sociological considerations is not entitled to the great weight ordinarily given the judgments based upon strictly military considerations." Against the arguments of urgent necessity advanced by the government's attorneys he set the fairly leisurely pace with which the evacuation had proceeded and the fact that "conditions were not such as to warrant a declaration of martial law." Nor could he forbear contrasting the manner in which the English in 1940 had examined 74,000 enemy aliens individually and that in

50

which Americans in 1942 had declined to make any attempt to separate the loyal from the disloyal in the Japanese-American population. To him the whole scheme was rankly unconstitutional and deserved to be labeled as such in the bluntest terms. "I dissent, therefore, from this legalization of racism."

Finally, Justice Jackson:

It would be impracticable and dangerous idealism to expect or insist that each specific military command in an area of probable operations will conform to conventional tests of constitutionality. When an area is so beset that it must be put under military control at all, the paramount consideration is that its measures be successful, rather than legal. . . . No court can require such a commander in such circumstances to act as a reasonable man; he may be unreasonably cautious and exacting. Perhaps he should be.

In short, the Court had no power to obstruct this unconstitutional program. At the same time, Jackson palliated this abdication of judicial oversight of military power by remarking that "If we cannot confine military expedients by the Constitution, neither would I distort the Constitution to approve all that the military may prove expedient." The fact that the courts could not prevent the execution of this program did not mean that they were therefore bound to lend a hand in enforcing it. Murphy and Roberts, in disapproving the evacuation, were wasting their time; the majority justices, in approving it, were creating a "loaded weapon ready for the hand of any authority that can bring forward a plausible claim of an urgent need." The correct thing to do, Jackson seemed to say, was to ignore the whole affair. "I should hold that a

51

civil court cannot be made to enforce an order which violates constitutional limitations even if it is a reasonable exercise of military authority." [44]

It would be easy to write ten or twenty or a hundred pages on the many astounding aspects of the great evacuation—the long history of prejudice against the Japanese-Americans, the economic and social pressures behind the demands for their removal, the mind of General DeWitt as laid bare in his own reports and those of investigating committees, the all but unanimous support tendered the Army by local and state officials, the time schedule, the actual record (which is no record at all) of espionage and sabotage on the Pacific coast, the recent efforts to do justice to these people, and a dozen other points of interest or incredulity. It would be easier still to analyze the various opinions in these three cases sentence by sentence, an exercise in judicial semantics, constitutional interpretation, and moral confusion that no student of the Court should fail to tackle. But that is not the purpose of these recollections of the evacuation. Their purpose is simply to evaluate the role of the judiciary, and especially that of the highest court, in this amazing assertion of presidential power. What are the lessons of these three cases?

In the first place, the very fact of this evacuation should be convincing proof that the courts of the United States, from highest to lowest, can do nothing to restrain and next to nothing to mitigate an arbitrary presidential-military program suspending the liberties of some part of

[44] 323 U.S. 243–248. Compare the dissent of Justice Rutledge in *Yakus v. U.S.*, 321 U.S. 414, 460–489 (1944), especially his thoughts at 467–468.

the civilian population, even when it takes months to carry through. There was no court, no writ, no show of judicial power that could be expected to check the President, Secretary Stimson, General DeWitt, or any of his officers in the immediate execution of this dictatorial decision to clear a racial minority out of an area announced to be "threatened with enemy invasion." This, then, is a first lesson of the evacuation: The courts are powerless to prevent a President from going into action with his powers of martial rule. And a second lesson, the inevitable result of the slowness of the judicial process, the difficulties in the path of an aggrieved individual bent on speedy relief, and the impossibility that one writ of injunction or even ten could halt an operation on this scale: The courts are likewise powerless to prevent him or his subordinates from carrying their plans through to conclusion. And a third lesson, which does little more than repeat what we have learned before: The courts will not, even when the necessity has clearly passed, presume to substitute their judgment for that of the military acting under presidential orders. Whatever relief is afforded, and however ringing the defense of liberty that goes with it, will be precious little and far too late.

The fact is that *Korematsu v. United States* makes perfect hash of the general principles of *Ex parte Milligan*. There was no suspension of the writ of habeas corpus, no declaration of martial law, no trial by military commission. But there was something that cut even deeper into the liberties of the American people: the wholesale invasion, based on a racial criterion, of the freedom of person of 70,000 citizens, an invasion of American liberty made all the more reprehensible, as Justice Murphy pointed out, by the fact that there was indeed no occasion for martial law. Nor can much stock be placed in the Court's numerous efforts to tie the whole program up with the string of the Act of March 21 into a conclusive bundle labeled "the war powers of the United States." From start to finish this was a naked display of the President's power of martial rule. The law in question simply made it easier to deal with the tiny handful of Japanese-Americans who were not overpowered by DeWitt's show of force. The Army could just as easily have "gone and got" Korematsu and hauled him off to Utah. And certainly Justice Jackson had no illusions that a refusal by the Court to help enforce the exclusion orders would in any way have cramped the general's style.

Again, perhaps, we have been too harsh with the Court. The majority justices would not use hindsight on the President and the Army; we should not use it on them. It should suffice to state the facts as they indubitably exist: The government of the United States, in a case of military necessity proclaimed by the President, and a fortiori when Congress has registered agreement, can be just as much a dictatorship, after its own fashion, as any other government on earth. The Supreme Court of the United States will not, and cannot be expected to, get in the way of this power.

Martial Law in Honolulu and Military Seizure in Chicago

The story of martial law in Hawaii is considerably less disturbing and has a slightly happier ending than the tribulations of the Japanese-Americans.[45] On December 7, 1941, for reasons that need no explanation, Governor J. B. Poindexter, acting upon a clear grant of authority in section 67 of the Organic Act of the Territory of Hawaii,[46] suspended the writ of habeas corpus, declared martial law throughout the islands, and turned over to the Commanding General, Hawaiian Department, the exercise of all his normal powers "during the present emergency and until the danger of invasion is removed." In conformance with the requirements of the statutory grant, a message was rushed off to President Roosevelt asking for approval of this action, and confirmation was immediately forthcoming. Through this action the President took full legal and constitutional responsibility for the initiation of military government.

The regime of martial law thus instituted was no mere paper transfer of power. The military assumed the entire governance of the islands. The civil authorities who continued to function did so at the pleasure and for the convenience of a military command that was legally and actually superior to them. The manner in which criminal justice was administered will be illustration enough. The Army took over courtrooms and offices; dispensed with such trappings as grand jury indictments, trial by jury, and rules of evidence; and handled criminal cases by summary procedure. There was no slackening in this regime until March, 1943, when the strong protests of Governor

[45] The literature on this subject is voluminous. See Rossiter, *Constitutional Dictatorship*, 284, and references there cited. Charles Fairman, "The Supreme Court on Military Jurisdiction," *Harvard Law Review*, LIX (1946), 833–882, especially 834–866, leaves virtually nothing to be said.
[46] 31 *Stat.* 141, 153.

Ingram M. Stainback, who had in the meantime replaced Poindexter, finally persuaded the military to restore eighteen functions of civil government to the regular authorities, although with the reserved right to resume them at any time. The important features of military law continued, however, with most crimes being tried by military courts. Despite a rising wave of criticism, especially after the Battle of Midway and the commencement of the great offensives eighteen months later, the state of martial law was not finally terminated until October 24, 1944, when a presidential proclamation cut short a regime that the military would just as soon have prolonged until the end of the war.[47]

With the writ of habeas corpus suspended, the civil courts of the territory, although fully prepared to perform their normal tasks, were powerless to give relief to the hundreds of civilians who were punished for the usual run of crimes and misdemeanors by military courts and summary procedures—powerless, that is, until a doughty district judge named Delbert E. Metzger got tired of waiting and in August, 1943, issued a writ of habeas corpus in the case of two naturalized Germans interned by the Army.[48] Lieutenant General Robert C. Richardson, then in command of the area, countered with an order, with penalties attached, forbidding any judge in the islands to

[47] 9 *Fed. Reg.* 12831.

[48] For the facts of this seriocomic episode, see Garner Anthony, "Martial Law, Military Government and the Writ of Habeas Corpus in Hawaii," *California Law Review,* XXXI (1943), 486 ff. Anthony, Attorney General of the Territory, was counsel for Duncan in the Supreme Court. See also Claude McColloch, "Now It Can Be Told," *American Bar Association Journal,* XXXV (1949), 365–368, 444–448.

entertain a petition for a writ of habeas corpus and incidentally naming Mctzgcr specifically. The judge, who had apparently been reading up on the Hall-Jackson vendetta at New Orleans in 1815, followed through with his grand riposte: a $5000 fine ($4000 more than Hall fined Jackson) for contempt of court! This head-on collision of determined exponents of two widely differing views of the Constitution was finally resolved by a compromise worked out by special emissaries of Attorney General Biddle and Secretary Stimson, through which the President remitted the fine (reduced to $100) and the general withdrew his order. The territorial courts were empowered to issue writs of habeas corpus, but prisoners were to gain release only on successful appeal to higher courts.

It was thus in early 1944 that two civilians—White, who had been convicted by a military tribunal in August, 1942, on a charge of embezzling stock, and Duncan, who had been similarly convicted in March, 1944, on a charge of assaulting two Marine sentries in the Pearl Harbor Navy Yard—were able to petition the territorial district court for writs of habeas corpus.[49] In each instance the district

[49] There had been one earlier attempt to challenge the military regime. Hans Zimmerman, a citizen arbitrarily detained by the Army, had sued unsuccessfully in February, 1942, for a writ of habeas corpus in the territorial court. Although he was locked up, his wife was free, and managed to get a review of his case in the circuit court (9th circuit) on the mainland. Failing to get a reversal, 132 Fed. 2d 442 (1942), she pushed on to the Supreme Court. On March 3, 1943, the Army removed Zimmerman to San Francisco and there, March 12, the day before she applied for a writ of certiorari, released him unconditionally. The Solicitor General brought this to the Court's attention, and the Court held the case moot, *Zimmerman v. Walker*, 319 U.S. 744 (1943). The possibilities of this road to freedom from military imprisonment were not further explored, but one man at least had gone up it to victory.

court held that the trials had been without authority and that the prisoners were entitled to their freedom. These holdings were appealed in tandem to the circuit court and there reversed. The Supreme Court granted certiorari in early 1945, heard arguments in December, and finally handed down its decision February 25, 1946.[50]

The Court held 6–2 that the prisoners had been unlawfully tried by the military tribunals, but as ever the decision was confined to the narrowest possible scope. The gist of Justice Black's opinion for the majority was that the "martial law" authorized by section 67 of the Organic Act did not extend so far as to justify the trial of civilians by military commission when the civil courts were in fact fully prepared to function normally. In other words, the opinion of the majority was based on the construction of a statute and not, as Justice Murphy insisted in a concurring opinion that it should have been, on constitutional grounds. Chief Justice Stone concurred in the result, but went on record as granting a wider scope to section 67. Justice Burton, joined by Justice Frankfurter, announced his conviction that the military governor had not exceeded the permissible range of discretion under the circumstances shown to have existed. Burton even went so far as to state, "I am obliged to dissent from the majority of this Court and to sound a note of warning against the dangers of over-expansion of judicial control into the fields allotted by the Constitution to agencies of legislative and executive action."

The majority justices, in deciding that these military trials could not be brought within the meaning of section

[50] *Duncan v. Kahanamoku, White v. Steer,* 327 U.S. 304 (1946); 146 Fed. 2d 576 (1944).

67, had to go behind the testimony of the military authorities concerning the necessities of the moment, read the facts of life in Hawaii in 1942 and 1944 for themselves, and substitute their own judgment for that of the authorities—something they had refused to do in *Korematsu v. United States*. In that case they had accepted at face value what Justice Murphy termed "an accumulation of much of the misinformation, half-truths, and insinuations that for years have been directed against Japanese-Americans by people with racial and economic prejudices." In this case, as if stung by Murphy's bitter words, they accepted nothing. The question inevitably arises: What would they have decided in *Duncan v. Kahanamoku* a year or two years or three years earlier? The most that can be said for this case is that two men got some extremely belated relief and that the Court indirectly upheld the Constitution. But the people of Hawaii lived under martial law from December, 1941, to October, 1944.

The third spectacular display in World War II of the President's power of martial rule—the seizure before, during, and after hostilities of some sixty plants or industries in which labor disputes had impeded (or threatened to impede) the war effort—had nothing to do with habeas corpus, martial law, or military commissions. Nevertheless, the wartime commandeering of private industry may be properly treated as an instance, however extraordinary, of this presidential power, for it was as commander in chief, with the use of federal troops, that Presidents Roosevelt and Truman engaged in this severe practice.[51] Not

[51] For a more complete treatment of this power, see Clinton Rossiter, "The President and Labor Disputes," *Journal of Politics*, XI (1949), 100–105.

even the extreme exponents of the strong presidency have argued that the President holds this authority in time of peace.

Wartime seizure is a relatively new departure. In the first World War President Wilson seized factories or industries on two occasions, in each instance under a grant of statutory authority. It remained for Franklin D. Roosevelt to base this practice on the exalted plane of the President's constitutional authority. The pattern of presidential power was set in the very first seizure of the "unlimited national emergency," that of the North American Aviation plant in Inglewood, California, in June, 1941. The President announced that he was acting pursuant to the powers vested in him "by the Constitution and laws of the United States, as President of the United States and Commander in Chief of the Army and Navy of the United States." [52] Just what these laws were, and there were several, Mr. Roosevelt did not trouble to say. Both he and Mr. Truman generally cited all their authorities for seizure in one jumbled sentence, leaving it to the commentators to determine which was the most reliable in any particular case. In 1943 the President was specifically granted the power of seizure in section 3 of the controversial Smith-Connally (War Labor Disputes) Act,[53] but in view of his status as commander in chief and the numerous actions of this nature he had already taken on that basis, this grant was at best declaratory, even supererogatory. It should be pointed out that all but a few seizures were occasioned by employer or union defiance of the directives of the

[52] 6 *Fed. Reg.* 2777.
[53] 57 *Stat.* 163, passed over Mr. Roosevelt's veto. This act came to an automatic end June 30, 1947.

National War Labor Board and its predecessor, the National Defense Mediation Board.

Only once in the course of the war was this power challenged in the courts, with results that must be set down as extremely disappointing for the purposes of this study. On December 28, 1944, by order of the President,[54] the Secretary of War took possession of nine of the plants and facilities of Montgomery Ward and Company. This bold move, the climax of an ill-tempered struggle between the War Labor Board and Mr. Sewell Avery that had kept the nation entertained for almost three years, was accompanied by an action in the district court in Chicago for a declaratory judgment to establish the legality of the seizure and for an injunction forbidding Avery and his officers to interfere with the government's possession. Normally the government would not have bothered with this quest for judicial approval, but the well-known nature of Ward's business was so different from that of the other plants that had been seized that it was considered good policy to have a ruling.

Solicitor General McGrath's argument made two points: (1) that the seizure was justified under section 3 of the Smith-Connally Act, which had authorized the President in the event of a dispute to seize "any plant, mine, or facility equipped for the manufacture, production, or mining of any articles or materials which may be required for the war effort or which may be useful in connection therewith"; (2) that, even if Ward's could not be brought within this formula, the President could seize these prop-

[54] 9 *Fed. Reg.* 15079. See 40 *O.A.G.* 312, in support of the first seizure, for the Attorney General's views of the President's authority to do this.

erties "under his general war powers." Both of these contentions were rejected by Judge Philip L. Sullivan on the general distinction, for which he consulted several dictionaries, that Ward's was engaged in "distribution" and not "production." His interpretation of the President's war powers was something less than Rooseveltian.[55]

The circuit court reversed this decision by a 2–1 vote. Again the question was: Does "production" include "distribution" within the meaning of the Smith-Connally Act? This time, after a slightly more careful examination of the statutory and judicial precedents, the answer was *yes*.[56] The court did not find it necessary to decide whether the President could have seized Montgomery Ward simply in his capacity as commander in chief, although it made no bones about its interest in this momentous question. "Active participation in its decision is intriguing," said Judge Evans, while refusing to be tempted from his secure position.

Certiorari was granted by the Supreme Court November 5, 1945, but hopes for a full rehearsal of the great arguments for and against Mr. Roosevelt's reading of his war powers, and for a major judicial pronouncement on this still unsettled question, were dashed by the Court's agreement with the Solicitor General that the case was moot.[57] The properties had been turned back to Mr.

[55] 58 Fed. Supp. 408 (1945).

[56] 150 Fed. 2d 369 (1945).

[57] *Montgomery Ward and Co. v. U.S.*, 326 U.S. 690 (1945). Certiorari had been denied at the previous term of court, 324 U.S. 858 (1945), on the ground that "application has been made prior to judgment of the Circuit Court of Appeals." It is also interesting to note that on the occasion of the government's first seizure of Montgomery Ward, in 1944, the properties were returned the day

Avery October 18, 1945. The Supreme Court's decision was vigorously protested by counsel for the company, who were anxious for a trial of strength in their own interest and in that of "a dispassionate review of one of the most ominous invasions of civil liberties which the late conflict encouraged," [58] but to no avail.

It is not likely that the Court would have held against the government in this important case. Undoubtedly it would have confined its attention to section 3 of the Smith-Connally Act and, having agreed with the circuit court that Montgomery Ward's business could be brought within its terms, avoided any statement concerning the President's constitutional war powers. Nor can there be any doubt that under the conditions of modern war the President has a broad constitutional power to seize and operate industrial facilities in which production has been halted, a power which, like his other powers of martial rule, is virtually impossible to define or control. Certainly it extends far into civilian territory, in view of the government's contention in the course of this litigation that the company deserved seizure because its defiance of the War Labor Board's orders threatened "the disintegration of the wartime structure of labor relations which . . . cannot survive successful repudiation by a company of the size and economic importance of Montgomery Ward." The activities of Mr. Roosevelt and inadequacies of the

before the district court was to announce a decision on the government's prayer for an injunction—thus rendering the case moot. For a somewhat similar case in World War I, see *Commercial Cable Co. v. Burleson*, 250 U.S. 360 (1919).

[58] *Memorandum on Behalf of Montgomery Ward and Company*, In the Supreme Court of the United States, October Term, 1945, No. 408, 7.

courts have forged yet another weapon of presidential martial power.

There is little to say in conclusion to this extended account of the judicial history of the President's power of martial rule, especially in the light of the estimates already voiced in connection with *Ex parte Merryman, Ex parte Milligan,* and *Korematsu v. United States.* There are many questions that go still unanswered—Can the President suspend the writ of habeas corpus? Can he declare martial law as a precautionary measure? Can he seize *any* plant that defies the decisions of his presidential wartime boards? Can he intern or evacuate citizens at his discretion?—but they are questions concerning the details of presidential power rather than its sweep, which the Court itself has acknowledged to be tremendous.

And if Lincoln and Roosevelt used this power without regard to the Court, what of the first President to face an atomic war? The only restrictions upon him as he invokes the fateful authority of martial rule will be his own political and moral sense, "the forbearance of a distracted people," [59] and the judgments of history. And *Ex parte Milligan* is proof enough that the judgments of the Court do not necessarily serve as the judgments of history.

[59] W. A. Dunning, *Essays on the Civil War and Reconstruction* (New York, 1898), 15.

PART II

The Supreme Court and Other
Aspects of the War Powers

Ex parte Milligan and *Korematsu v. United States,*
dramatic and controversial as they may be, by no means
tell the whole story of judicial review of the war powers.
There have been at least five other perplexing constitutional questions—Who can start a war? When is a war
"over," and who is to end it? What are the war powers of
Congress, and to what extent may they be delegated to
the President? How independent of the Supreme Court
are courts-martial and presidential military commissions?
What are the President's powers in conquered areas?—
that the Court has been begged to answer with some show
of finality. Let us see if the Court has acted any more
boldly and clearheadedly in dealing with these problems
than it has in pronouncing the law of martial rule.

The President's Power to Wage
Defensive War

One of the truly unique provisions of the American
Constitution is the clause that confides to an independent
legislature the power "to declare war." The Senate's

searching debate in 1949 over the implications of article 5 of the North Atlantic Pact served as a dramatic reminder of this canon of our constitutional system: that the nation cannot be finally and constitutionally committed to a state of war without the positive approval of both houses of Congress.[1]

At the same time, it is a matter of history that most of our wars were in full course before Congress could get around to declaring the fact, and it has therefore always been assumed that the President, as commander in chief, could order the armed services to "meet force with force." [2] The extent of his powers of defensive war remains a much-argued problem, however, and Congresses, Courts, commentators, and even Presidents [3] have experienced con-

[1] But of course the President could veto a declaration of war, something that Cleveland for one was probably quite ready to do—in the case of war with Spain. See generally S. E. Baldwin, "The Share of the President of the United States in a Declaration of War," *American Journal of International Law*, XII (1918), 1–14.

[2] See the exhaustive discussion of this problem in C. A. Berdahl, *War Powers of the Executive* (Urbana, Ill., 1922), chap. 4, and the various works cited in his notes. See also T. S. Woolsey, "The Beginnings of War," *Proceedings of the American Political Science Association*, I (1904), 54–68; A. H. Putney, "Executive Assumption of the War Making Power," *National University Law Review*, VII, No. 2 (1927), 1–41; C. C. Tansill, "War Powers of the President of the United States with Special Reference to the Beginning of Hostilities," *Political Science Quarterly*, XLV (1930), 1–55; J. B. Moore, *Digest of International Law* (Washington, 1906), VII, 162–172.

[3] Particularly Jefferson, as might be expected. See his faint-hearted message to Congress, December 8, 1801, Richardson, *op. cit.*, I, 327, as well as a second message, December 6, 1805, *ibid.*, 388–390. Hamilton's scornful and realistic comment on Jefferson's doubts is in his *Works*, H. C. Lodge, ed. (New York, 1886), VII, 200–206.

siderable difficulty in fixing the boundaries of his power to fight without a declaration and in answering the important legal question, "When is the United States in a state of war as regards neutral rights, other third-party interests, the operation of wartime statutes, and other such matters?"

The framers of the Constitution, who had some first-hand knowledge of this sort of thing, recognized frankly that this nation could be embroiled in major hostilities without an express declaration. On August 17, 1787, in the course of a debate whether Congress should be given the power "to make war," Madison and Gerry "moved to insert 'declare,' striking out 'make' war; leaving to the Executive the power to repel sudden attacks," and the motion was carried.[4] The need for executive defensive action was also acknowledged in the militia clause (Art. I, sec. 18, cl. 15), as well as in statutes of 1792 and 1795 empowering the President to call forth the militia in actual or threatened invasion.[5]

The subsequent history of the Republic has justified the prescience of the framers and early legislators, for we have several times been factually and even legally at war without an express declaration by Congress. In at least four instances—1798–1800, 1801–1805, 1815, and 1914–1917—we have fought a public war without any declaration at all.[6] Generally, however, Congress has been only too will-

[4] Max Farrand, ed., *Records of the Federal Convention* (New Haven, Conn., 1911), II, 318–319.

[5] 1 *Stat.* 264, 424.

[6] See generally J. G. Rogers, *World Policing and the Constitution* (Boston, 1945), 45–55. In *Hamilton v. McLaughry*, 136 Fed. 445, 449–450 (1905), the period of the Boxer Rebellion was held to be a "time of war" within the meaning of the 58th Article of War.

ing to acknowledge by declarative resolution that war has been thrust upon us, and has expressly or by implication approved the acts of war for which the President's power as commander in chief was up to that moment the sole constitutional justification.

Fortunately for commentators and constitutional historians, as well as for Presidents anxious for impeccable judicial support for their more questionable acts of defensive war, there is a major Supreme Court decision favoring the President on this very point. Even more fortunately, the decision was not unanimous, and limitationists have hardly less impeccable precedents of their own to cite in defense of strict construction of the war-declaring power.[7] The decision, easily one of the most momentous in the history of the Court's interpretation of presidential power, was the celebrated *Prize Cases*, argued before the Court February 10–25 and announced March 10, 1863.[8] In this instance the Court was brought face to face with one of the most controversial actions of Lincoln's great eleven-week "dictatorship," the blockade of

---

See also *Thomas v. U.S.*, 39 Ct. Cls. 1, 6–9 (1903), and *Warner, Barnes and Co. v. U.S.*, 40 Ct. Cls. 1, 28–30 (1904), in which the Philippine Insurrection was likewise held to be a public war.

[7] Note the weight that Willoughby accords the dissent in his *Constitutional Law*, III, 1559–1560. The most recent authoritative statement of the limited view of the President's warmaking powers is that of Senator Taft, delivered June 28, 1950, at the beginning of the Korean crisis. See *Daily Congressional Record*, 9460–9461. The advocates of untrammeled presidential power rely heavily on Nelson's opinion in *Durand v. Hollins*, 4 Blatch. 451 (1860), which sustained Pierce's authorization to a naval commander to bombard Greytown, Nicaragua, in retaliation for a mob assault on the American consul. Had this litigation been decided in the Supreme Court, it would have been one of the four or five leading cases in this book.

[8] 2 Black 635 (1863).

the Confederacy effected by his proclamations of April 19 and 27, 1861.[9] Four ships—two American, one Mexican, one British—had been captured by Union naval vessels enforcing the blockade and had been brought into various ports to be libeled as prizes. "The libels were filed by the proper District Attorneys, on behalf of the United States and on behalf of the officers and crews of the ships, by which the captures were respectively made. In each case the District Court pronounced a decree of condemnation, from which the claimants took an appeal." Once again the capricious mechanics of "government by lawsuit" had forced the Supreme Court to decide the constitutional validity of an important exercise of presidential power. Indeed, the problem of public policy before the Court was even more sweeping than that, for as counsel for one of the shipowners boldly reminded the justices, "The question here is, how can the United States, under the Constitution, be involved in war?"

The complexities of this great case attracted much popular attention. More important, they attracted a display of legal and forensic talent rarely equaled in the history of the Court, nine ornaments of the bar—including Attorney General Bates, William M. Evarts, James M. Carlisle, and Richard Henry Dana (who had learned the law of the sea the hard way)—all fully prepared to range far and wide upon the law of nations, the war powers of the President, and the legal subtleties of "intestine conflict." The arguments, which consumed twelve full days of the Court's unforced attention, make exciting reading even today. For eloquence, passion, and depth of learning they have never been surpassed in our judicial history.

The Court was faced with a personal problem of no

[9] 12 *Stat.* 1258, 1259.

little magnitude. For one thing, its stock of popular support had never been lower; the ghost of Dred Scott would not be laid. For another, the peculiar nature of this case and the war that had produced it made certain that, no matter what the decision, the Court would not please everybody and might not please anybody. The possibilities of this situation have been graphically stated by Taney's biographer:

> The Supreme Court was in a position greatly to embarrass the government in either of two ways. It might hold that the conflict was not a war and not covered by the laws of war, and that the prizes had been illegally taken and foreign trade with southern ports illegally broken up. Such a position would make the government liable for huge sums in damages, and its psychological effect would be such as seriously to cripple the conduct of the war. On the other hand the court might hold that the Confederacy was an independent sovereign power, and, although holding the blockade to be legal, it might do it in such a way as to encourage the recognition of the Confederacy by foreign governments. Such a decision would be only less serious than the other.[10]

The Court escaped neatly but narrowly from this beckoning trap. To the precise question for which the justices agreed to find an answer—"Had the President a right to institute a blockade of ports in possession of persons in armed rebellion against the Government, on the principles of international law, as known and acknowledged among civilized States?"—five judges (Grier, Wayne, and the three Lincoln appointees then on the Court, Swayne, Miller, and Davis) answered *yes;* four (Nelson, Clifford,

[10] Swisher, *Taney,* 563–564. Quoted by permission of the Macmillan Company.

70

Catron, and Taney) answered *no*. The heart of Grier's decision was his belief that the insurrection of the southern states was a "state of war" in contemplation of domestic and international law, and that the President's proclamation of blockade and the capture of these prizes were therefore entirely legitimate. At the same time that he accorded the Union full belligerent rights from the beginning of the insurrection, he did not accord any rights of sovereignty to the South, even by implication. This, of course, was the extraordinary conception of the nature of this conflict to which Lincoln had come at an early date. He could not have asked for a more favorable opinion.

The essential passages of Grier's opinion, quoted hundreds of times since by champions of the strong presidency, are these:

If a war be made by invasion of a foreign nation, the President is not only authorized but bound to resist force by force. He does not initiate the war, but is bound to accept the challenge without waiting for any special legislative authority. And whether the hostile party be a foreign invader, or States organized in rebellion, it is nonetheless a war, although the declaration of it be *"unilateral."* . . .

This greatest of civil wars was not gradually developed by popular commotion, tumultuous assemblies, or local unorganized insurrections. However long may have been its previous conception, it nevertheless sprung forth suddenly from the parent brain, a Minerva in the full panoply of *war*. The President was bound to meet it in the shape it presented itself, without waiting for Congress to baptize it with a name; and no name given to it by him or them could change the fact. . . .

Whether the President in fulfilling his duties, as Commander-in-chief, in suppressing an insurrection, has met with such armed hostile resistance, and a civil war of such alarming proportions as will compel him to accord to them the character of belligerents, is a question to be decided *by him,* and this Court must be governed by the decisions and acts of the political department of the Government to which this power was entrusted. "He must determine what degree of force the crisis demands." The proclamation of blockade is itself official and conclusive evidence to the Court that a state of war existed which demanded and authorized a recourse to such a measure, under the circumstances peculiar to the case.[11]

At one point in his opinion Grier turned aside to observe, with some show of irritation, that these third parties could hardly ask the Court "to affect a technical ignorance of the existence of a war, which all the world acknowledges to be the greatest civil war known in the history of the human race, and thus cripple the arm of the Government and paralyze its power by subtle definition and ingenious sophisms." [12] The expression "subtle definition and ingenious sophisms" is worth quoting and remembering. It sums up neatly not only the character of Nelson's dissenting opinion but also the whole history of this extraordinary process, repeated in every one of our wars, through which injured private interests have set out to embarrass the war power of the United States in the hope of personal redress. The great legal arguments over the extent of this power have been carried on not between opposing branches of the government with national ends in view, but between a government anxious to enforce its laws and private persons anxious to evade their admittedly

[11] 2 Black 668–670. See also *Matthews v. McStea,* 91 U.S. 7, 12–13 (1875).
[12] 2 Black 669–670.

harsh application. Subtle definition and ingenious sophisms have been the chief weapons of these interests since
time out of mind.

In this particular instance the dissenting justices agreed
with Carlisle's brilliant, if entirely too legalistic, argument that "war did not exist; blockade did not exist; and
there could be no capture for breach of blockade, or in-
tent to break it." Not everything the President had done
to meet the insurrection had been illegal. He was certainly
empowered to wage war upon the rebels "under the municipal laws of the country," but he could not take any
action "under the law of nations." He could march his
legions up and down the South, but he could not, no matter how many supply ships were sailing in and out of
Confederate ports, proclaim a blockade that neutral third
parties were bound to respect—not until Congress had
recognized the situation through a declaration of war.
This step had not been taken, Nelson asserted, until the
Act of July 13, 1861.[13] Prizes taken between April 19 and
that date could not be libeled in the courts of the United
States. In short, the President could "meet the adversary
upon land and water with all the forces of the Government," but not with all the forces of the law!

The telling passages of Nelson's opinion are these:

> Now, in one sense, no doubt this is war, and may be a war
> of the most extensive and threatening dimensions and effects,
> but it is a statement simply of its existence in a material sense,
> and has no relevancy or weight when the question is what
> constitutes a war in a legal sense, in the sense of the law of
> nations, and of the Constitution of the United States? For it
> must be a war in this sense to attach to it all the consequences

[13] 12 *Stat.* 255.

that belong to belligerent rights. Instead, therefore, of inquiring after armies and navies, and victories lost and won, or organized rebellion against the general Government, the inquiry should be into the law of nations and into the municipal fundamental laws of the Government. For we find there that to constitute a civil war in the sense in which we are speaking, before it can exist, in contemplation of law, it must be recognized or declared by the sovereign power of the States, and which sovereign power by our Constitution is lodged in the Congress of the United States. . . .

So the war carried on by the President against the insurrectionary districts in the Southern States, as in the case of the King of Great Britain in the American Revolution, was a personal war against those in rebellion, . . . with this difference, as the war-making power belonged to the king, he might have recognized or declared the war at the beginning to be a civil war . . . , but in the case of the President no such power existed: the war therefore from necessity was a personal war, until Congress assembled and acted upon this state of things. . . .

I am compelled to the conclusion . . . that the President does not possess the power under the Constitution to declare war or recognize its existence within the meaning of the law of nations, which carries with it belligerent rights, and thus change the country and all its citizens from a state of peace to a state of war.[14]

What then can we say of the decision in the *Prize Cases* and its significance for the President's military powers? For Lincoln, the result and the majority opinion were entirely satisfactory. Nelson's opinion, too, was no balm to the South and, as an isolated instance of minority judicial disapproval of certain phases of the war, of little more

[14] 2 Black 690, 694–695, 698.

satisfaction to Lincoln's detractors. In particular Lincoln was encouraged to believe that his ever-broadening interpretation of the commander-in-chief clause would encounter no substantial restrictions in the future decisions of the Court. It was a fact of considerable importance for the conduct of the war that the Court, although clearly in a position to do all sorts of legal and moral damage to the cause, did not go out of its way to castigate Lincoln's theory of his powers (as expounded by Dana) or invite other challenges to the effective prosecution of the war. Although direct evidence on the subject is impossible to find, it seems reasonable to believe that the *Prize Cases* went far to discourage determined assaults on the validity of the Conscription Act of 1863, the Legal Tender Act of 1862, the Emancipation Proclamation, and the various arbitrary suspensions of free speech and press, all of which were considered palpably unconstitutional by Chief Justice Taney.[15] The decision in the *Prize Cases* was a welcome addition to the arguments of the Union men, and Lincoln fought his war with no more thought about the Supreme Court than was necessary in making his five appointments.

For future occasions when Presidents would be forced to fight without prior congressional authorization, the case was as important as a case can be in shaping the contours of presidential power, especially since there have been no further decisions on this tremendous constitutional and practical problem.[16] After the two points of

[15] Swisher, *Taney*, 566–572.

[16] For the Court's opinion on the date of commencement of the Spanish-American War, see *The Pedro*, 175 U.S. 354, 363 (1899); for World War II, see E. M. Borchard, "When Did the War Begin," *Columbia Law Review*, XLVII (1947), 742–748. In *New*

view of the *Prize Cases,* which can certainly be expanded into general theories of the President's authority in foreign as well as domestic war, there is really little more to be said. The split in the Court was a pretty accurate reflection then, and remains one now, of the division of informed opinion on an unsettled question. In this case, as in so many others, the two views of the Constitution—as grant of power and as catalogue of limitations—clashed head on. Five of the judges were, for various reasons, thinking in terms of power, four in terms of limitations, and probably all nine would just as soon have found some middle ground.

Yet war, even as fought by the constitutional Americans, always has been a question of power, and it seems more than providential that the decision, however closely fought, should have been in favor of the Union rather than the Constitution. In the final analysis, the facts of history and the doctrine of the *Prize Cases* dovetail rather neatly, and both bear impressive witness to the cogency of Richard Henry Dana's sweeping view of presidential warmaking powers in his argument for the United States:

It is not necessary to the exercise of war powers by the President, in a case of foreign war, that there should be a preceding act of Congress declaring war.

The Constitution gives to Congress the power to declare war.

But there are two parties to a war. War is *a state of things,* and not an act of legislative will. If a foreign power springs

---

York Life Insurance Co. v. Bennion, 158 Fed. 2d 260 (1946), it was held, for purposes of construction of a life insurance policy, that the war began legally with the Japanese attack on Pearl Harbor. Certiorari in this case was denied by the Supreme Court, 331 U.S. 811 (1947).

76

a war upon us by sea and land, during a recess of Congress, exercising all belligerent rights of capture, the question is, whether the President can repel war with war . . . or whether that would be illegal? . . .

It is enough to state the proposition. If it be not so, there is no protection to the State.[17]

Yet Carlisle, the opposing counsel, in summing up Dana's argument, and therefore overstating it for effect, was an even better if unwitting prophet for war in the atomic age:

The matter then comes . . . to the pure question of the power of the President under the Constitution. And this is, perhaps, the most extraordinary part of the argument for the United States. It is founded upon a figure of speech, which is repugnant to the genius of republican institutions, and, above all, to our written Constitution. It makes the President, in some sort, the impersonation of the country, and invokes for him the power and right to use all the forces he can command to *save the life of the nation.* The principle of self-defense is asserted, and all power is claimed for the President. This is to assert that the Constitution contemplated and tacitly provided that the President should be dictator, and all constitutional government be at an end whenever he should think that "the life of the nation" is in danger.[18]

The Supreme Court's Lack of Power
to Declare Peace

In sharp contrast to the clear-cut words of the Constitution on the power to declare war is its casual silence on the power to make peace. The failure of the framers to

[17] 2 Black 659–660.
[18] 2 Black 648.

include a positive statement of the location of this power was not entirely accidental, for Madison's *Journal* records that on August 17, 1787, Pierce Butler's motion to add the words "and peace" after the words "to declare war" was voted down unanimously [19]—principally, as Story was later to write, "upon the plain ground that it [the power to make peace] more properly belonged to the treaty-making power." [20] It seems clear that an overwhelming majority of the framers considered that the power to make peace was first of all lodged with President and Senate in their treaty-making capacity.

As a matter of historical practice the government of the United States has "declared peace" by several methods other than that of the solemn constitutional treaty, although the latter has always remained the most important technique. A recent opinion of the Supreme Court acknowledges that a state of war "may be terminated by treaty or legislation or Presidential proclamation," [21] and adds significantly, "Whatever the mode, its termination is a political act." Thus the Court at one time or another has given full support to the action of the political branches in terminating war by treaty (the Spanish-American War),[22] by proclamation of the President (the

---

[19] Farrand, *op. cit.*, II, 319, also 540–541.

[20] *Commentaries*, sec. 1173.

[21] *Ludecke v. Watkins*, 335 U.S. 160, 168–169 (1948).

[22] *Hijo v. U.S.*, 194 U.S. 315, 323 (1904). In *MacLeod v. U.S.*, 229 U.S. 416, 432 (1913), the Court stated that "a state of war as to third persons continued until the exchange of treaty ratifications." On treaties of peace, see also *Haver v. Yaker*, 9 Wallace 32 (1869); *U.S. v. Anderson*, 9 Wallace 56, 70 (1869); *Dooley v. U.S.*, 182 U.S. 222, 230 (1901).

Civil War),[23] and by joint resolution (World War I).[24] Nor does this exhaust the techniques of peacemaking that could be constitutionally employed—employed, that is to say, by the President and tolerated as a "political act" by the Court. An executive agreement with or without specific congressional authorization would seem one way to end a war, should the political-international situation demand such action; Congress could also authorize the President to proclaim the official termination of a state of

[23] It was held several times by the Court that the Civil War ended on two different dates in two different parts of the South— by presidential proclamation of April 2, 1866 (14 *Stat.* 811), in all states except Texas, and by proclamation of August 20, 1866 (14 *Stat.* 814), in the latter state. See especially *The Protector*, 12 Wallace 700, 702 (1871), as to the legal dates for the beginning and ending of the war. See also *Masterson v. Howard*, 18 Wallace 99, 105–106 (1873), and *Burke v. Miltenberger*, 19 Wallace 519, 525 (1873). The power of the President to terminate a foreign war by proclamation is a question to which the future alone can offer a satisfactory answer. It is important to note that President Wilson denied categorically that he possessed any such power. See his letter to Senator Fall, printed in the *New York Times*, August 22, 1919, 2. For sound comment on this problem, see J. M. Mathews, "The Termination of War," *Michigan Law Review*, XIX (1921), 833–834.

[24] The famed joint resolution of July 2, 1921 (42 *Stat.* 105; see also 41 *Stat.* 1359), was accorded full respect by the Court in *Commercial Trust Co. v. Miller*, 262 U.S. 51, 57 (1923); *Swiss Insurance Co. v. Miller*, 267 U.S. 42 (1925); and many similar cases. For a fuller ventilation of the constitutional problems involved in making peace, see Berdahl, *War Powers*, chap. 14; Willoughby, *Constitutional Law*, I, 534–536; E. S. Corwin, "The Power of Congress to Declare Peace," *Michigan Law Review*, XVIII (1920), 669–675; Quincy Wright, *The Control of American Foreign Relations* (New York, 1922), 290–293; Coleman Phillipson, *Termination of War and Treaties of Peace* (New York, 1916).

war after ascertaining certain facts, in other words, largely at his own discretion. Something of this sort is to be found in several sections of certain important statutes enacted during the first World War.[25] And it is altogether possible, especially in this atomic age, that an enemy would be so completely reduced to a state of impotent anarchy as to leave no authority with which we could negotiate a peace. In such an eventuality the President or Congress, or preferably both, would probably make an official statement to this effect, which the courts would doubtless accord judicial recognition.[26] Finally, it need only be mentioned in passing that the power to terminate actual hostilities by an armistice or other agreement is a strictly military power, belonging to the President as commander in chief, that no litigant has ever been so brazen as to question.

This reference to the President's power to negotiate an armistice should remind us that there is something more to war than war itself. Not only do we have the "war before the war"; more important, we have the war after it, a war than can "rage" for some years after the shooting has died down. This is a fact of huge consequence for the scope and effect of presidential power. No one could have lived through the years after World War II and failed to feel the effects of the vast power that has been left by the American people in the possession of their government, especially in the hands of the President, simply because they are still not at peace with Germany or Japan, or finished with the unlimited national emergency declared

[25] 40 *Stat.* 276, 283–284, 411, 412.

[26] The reverse of this situation, the *United States* in "impotent anarchy," is something about which we might also give a thought.

by President Roosevelt May 27, 1941. Reconversion and rent control are only two of the many areas into which the war power of Congress has continued to reach, while Mr. Truman has dealt with a variety of problems from Russian intransigeance to railroad strikes as a commander in chief with abnormal constitutional and statutory competence. To accept, as accept we must, the theory that every state of war extends for an indefinite number of years beyond the end of hostilities is to acquiesce in an immense expansion of national, congressional, and especially presidential power.

It is therefore highly important to record that the Supreme Court, although repeatedly requested to declare that occasion for the exercise of this or that war power had in fact ceased, has uniformly, if not altogether unanimously, favored the government's contention that war does not end with the last shot, nor for some years thereafter. A case or two from each of our last four major wars may be briefly examined to illustrate the Court's historic attitude on this currently debated question.

In *Stewart v. Kahn* [27] (1870) the Court, which in a variety of opinions had already announced or assumed that the Civil War continued until President Johnson's two proclamations of 1866, took special pains to remind the litigants that the war power of the United States "is not limited to victories in the field and the dispersion of the insurgent forces. It carries with it inherently the power to guard against the immediate renewal of the conflict, and to remedy the evils which have arisen from its rise and progress." The implications for presidential authority of

[27] 11 Wallace 493, 507 (1870). See also *The Protector*, 12 Wallace 700, 702 (1871).

81

this eminently practical doctrine are better imagined than specifically catalogued. It opens the door to an undefined and therefore virtually unlimited exercise of the war power after the war, with impact on enemy and citizen alike.

Hijo v. United States [28] affords ample evidence that Chief Justice Fuller and his election-following Court subscribed without reservation to the doctrine that war with Spain did not terminate until the exchange of ratifications of the Treaty of Paris in April, 1899. A Spanish corporation's contention that the war had ended with the protocol and presidential proclamation of August 12, 1898, suspending hostilities was met by Justice Harlan with passages from Kent's *Commentaries* brought to the Court's attention by Assistant Attorney General James Clark McReynolds.[29]

Hamilton v. Kentucky Distilleries and *Ruppert v. Caffey* [30] were the leading cases in which the Court was asked to re-examine this problem during the postwar years of World War I. It is the first of these that is generally cited as the basic case in this particular field; but the latter, too, invites our attention, chiefly because of the appearance for Ruppert's Beer of Mr. Elihu Root and his eloquent, and nearly successful, appeal to the shade of Lambdin P. Milligan. In addition, both these cases present a splendid example of the manner in which injured private

[28] 194 U.S. 315, 323 (1904). See also 22 *O.A.G.* 190.

[29] The passages in the *Commentaries* may be found in the second edition (New York, 1832), I, 159–161.

[30] 251 U.S. 146, 158–163, 165–168 (1919); 251 U.S. 264 (1920). See also *Commercial Cable Co. v. Burleson*, 255 Fed. 99, 104–106 (1919), which exhibits Judge Learned Hand at his learned best.

interests can force the Court to stand up and be counted on a major issue of national policy, even if most of the justices will say nothing more than "count us out."

The interests in these cases *had* been injured heavily, even disastrously. There could be no doubt of their right to a day in the highest court of the land, for the enforcement of one controversial law, enacted by Congress under the approving eye of President Wilson, meant, and was supposed to mean, nothing less than the indefinite and uncompensated suspension of their business. This, of course, was the famed War-Time Prohibition Act of November 22, 1918,[31] an exercise of the war power (ten days after the cessation of hostilities) that made it "unlawful to sell for beverage purposes any distilled spirits, . . . for the purpose of conserving the man power of the Nation, and to increase efficiency in the production of arms, munitions, ships, food, and clothing for the Army and Navy." Among the arguments put forward by the Kentucky Distilleries, which obviously represented every distillery in America, was the assertion that the act "became void before these suits were brought [October 10, 1919] by reason of the passing of the war emergency." A unanimous Court, speaking through Justice Brandeis, rejected this contention with force and finality. With approving references to *Hijo v. United States* and *Stewart v. Kahn*, as well as to the numerous postwar actions of President Wilson explainable only in terms of a continuing emergency, the Court refused to "enquire into the motives of Congress" or the "wisdom of the legislation."

In view of facts of public knowledge, . . . that the treaty of peace has not yet been concluded, that the railways are

[31] 40 *Stat.* 1045.

still under national control by virtue of the war powers, that other war activities have not been brought to a close, and that it cannot even be said that the man power of the nation has been restored to a peace footing, we are unable to conclude that the act has ceased to be valid.[32]

At the same time, Brandeis remarked "that it would require a clear case to justify a court in declaring that such an act, passed for such a purpose, had ceased to have force because the power of Congress no longer continued," a statement that seemed to leave other laws and presidential actions open to challenge. And in *Ruppert v. Caffey,* argued at the same time and decided only three weeks after *Hamilton v. Kentucky Distilleries,* four justices decided that the war power stopped short of Colonel Ruppert's beer. Justice McReynolds, a border-state gentleman who could tell bourbon from beer, summed up his opinion in this characteristic passage:

The argument runs—This court has held in *Hamilton v. Kentucky Distilleries* that under a power implied because necessary and proper to carry into execution the above named powers relating to war, in October, 1919, Congress could prohibit the sale of intoxicating liquors. In order to make such a prohibition effective the sale of non-intoxicating beer must be forbidden. Wherefore, from the implied power to prohibit intoxicants the further power to prohibit this non-intoxicant must be implied.

The query at once arises: If all this be true, why may not the second implied power engender a third under which Congress may forbid the planting of barley or hops, the manufacture of bottles or kegs, etc.? [33]

[32] 251 U.S. 163.
[33] 251 U.S. 305–306.

84

And with the aid of two full pages of *Ex parte Milligan* Justice McReynolds had no difficulty substituting his judgment for that of President and Congress in determining whether prohibition of nonintoxicating beer was a valid use of the war power one year after the cessation of hostilities. This, of course, was a very special case of that power interfering with a legitimate private interest, and these justices, troubled at the sight of a major industry singled out for annihilation under a strained reading of the war powers, simply decided that here was a proper place to call a halt. The only basis for distinguishing their stands in the Hamilton and Ruppert cases is that whiskey is one thing and beer another. On a variety of such distinctions is our jurisprudence grounded.

The pattern of World War I was repeated in the years after V-E and V-J Days. In two major cases, *Fleming v. Mohawk Wrecking and Lumber Co.* (April 28, 1947) and *Woods v. Miller Co.* (February 16, 1948),[34] the Court evidenced few qualms in rejecting the contentions of private interests that the war emergency had come to an end; in a third, *Ludecke v. Watkins* (June 21, 1948),[35] involving the arbitrary handling of an enemy alien under a sweeping and ancient statutory grant of presidential power, the Court decided only 5–4 in favor of the govern-

[34] 331 U.S. 111, 116 (1947); 333 U.S. 138, 141–147 (1948). See also *U.S. v. Shaugnessy*, 70 S. Ct. 309, 314, decided January 16, 1950. For informative recent comment on this problem, see Theodore French, "The End of the War," *George Washington Law Review*, XV (1947), 191–201, and the learned note—an outstanding example of what a good law-review note should be—"Judicial Determination of the End of War," *Columbia Law Review*, XLVII (1947), 255–268.

[35] 335 U.S. 160 (1948).

ment and questioned bluntly the unqualified existence of a state of war.

The exercise of war power under attack in the Fleming case was an executive order of December 12, 1946,[36] consolidating the OPA and three other agencies into the Office of Temporary Controls. The order was issued under authority of the First War Powers Act of 1941,[37] which granted the President a broad power of administrative reorganization "only in matters relating to the conduct of the present war" and "during the continuance of the present war and for six months after the termination of the war." The Court denied without dissent the argument of counsel for the Mohawk Company that President Truman's proclamation of a "cessation of hostilities" on December 31, 1946,[38] had ended the state of war. Full reliance was placed on *Hamilton v. Kentucky Distilleries* and *Stewart v. Kahn.* "The cessation of hostilities," said Justice Douglas, "does not necessarily end the war power. . . . Whatever may be the reach of that power, it is plainly adequate to deal with problems of law enforcement which arise during the period of hostilities but do not cease with them."

In *Woods v. Miller Co.* the exercise of war power was a far-reaching statute, the Housing and Rent Act of June 30, 1947,[39] passed by Congress more than twenty-two months after the last shot was fired. Again the Court found the war power sufficient. Said Justice Douglas:

[36] 11 *Fed. Reg.* 14281.
[37] 55 *Stat.* 838.
[38] 12 *Fed. Reg.* 1.
[39] 61 *Stat.* 193.

The legislative history of the present Act makes abundantly clear that there has not yet been eliminated the deficit in housing which in considerable measure was caused by the heavy demobilization of veterans and by the cessation or reduction in residential construction during the period of hostilities. . . . Since the war effort contributed heavily to that deficit, Congress has the power even after the cessation of hostilities to act to control the forces that a short supply of the needed article created. . . .

We recognize the force of the argument that the effects of war under modern conditions may be felt in the economy for years and years, and that if the war power can be used in days of peace to treat all the wounds which war inflicts on our society, it may not only swallow up all other powers of Congress but largely obliterate the Ninth and Tenth Amendments as well. There are no such implications in today's decision.[40]

Justice Jackson, in concurring, made even more articulate the Court's feeling that there must be some limit somewhere beyond which it would refuse to go in support of the war powers. "I cannot accept the argument that war powers last as long as the effects and consequences of war, for if so they are permanent—as permanent as the war debts." For Jackson the fact that "we have armies abroad exercising our war power and have made no peace terms with our allies, not to mention our principal enemies" was sufficient to justify this act and its enforcement.[41]

Finally, in *Ludecke v. Watkins*, some three years after the fighting had ended, the Court was forced to consider

[40] 333 U.S. 142–144.
[41] 333 U.S. 147.

the applicability of the Alien Enemy Act of 1798,[42] which gave the President broad authority to restrain and remove alien enemies "whenever there is a declared war between the United States and any foreign nation or government." The decision was 5–4 in favor of the government. The question of "war or no war?" was not presented or answered in a clear-cut manner, principally because the hard problems of civil liberty for alien enemies and of judicial review of administrative action were uppermost in the minds of the dissenting justices, but it did evoke significant comment. Said Justice Frankfurter in his majority opinion: "Whether and when it would be open to this Court to find that a war though merely kept formally alive had in fact ended, is a question too fraught with gravity even to be adequately formulated when not compelled." And the Liberal Four (Black, Douglas, Rutledge, and Murphy) rushed through this opened door to announce that the doctrine of *Stewart v. Kahn* and *Hamilton v. Kentucky Distilleries* could not be stretched to cover this set of facts. Said the first of these, "I think the idea that we are still at war with Germany in the sense contemplated by the statute controlling here is a pure fiction," and, "Whatever else that fiction might support, I refuse to agree that it affords a basis for today's holding that our laws authorize the peacetime banishment of any person on the judicially unreviewable conclusion of a single individual. The 1798 Act did not grant its extraordinary and dangerous powers to be used during the period of fictional wars."

Will the logic of this dissent ever appeal to a majority of the Court and thus serve as a check to the hitherto unbounded post-bellum sweep of the war powers? The an-

[42] 1 *Stat.* 577, as amended by 40 *Stat.* 531.

swer to this question would seem to be *yes*. In a case such as this, one in which the check upon the political branches would be confined to a particular exercise of the war power and would affect only the parties to the suit, it is altogether possible that the Court would refuse to accept the fiction of a state of war. But in a case in which an adverse decision would interfere on an important scale with the domestic and diplomatic policies of President and Congress or alter the rights of millions of individuals, it would be idle to expect the Court to go to the mat with the government. In other words, *Hamilton v. Kentucky Distilleries,* with all its implications for national and presidential power, remains good law and sound politics, while the dissents in *Ruppert v. Caffey* and *Ludecke v. Watkins* constitute a footnote to that case which may yet become a definite qualification. However that may be, the Court has yet to disagree officially with the President's lawyers on this momentous issue, and if it ever does, we can be sure that the case will be one with a narrow range. We cannot expect the Court to end our wars.[43]

Judicial Review of the War Powers of Congress

The President cannot conduct our wars simply on the basis of his constitutional authority as commander in chief. His powers of command are spacious, but first he must have something to command. Congress alone can supply the men, money, and munitions with which he pursues the success of our arms. He must also rely on the legislative will for all those supplementary statutory

[43] On the problem of emergency, see the interesting decision in *East New York Savings Bank v. Hahn,* 326 U.S. 230 (1945).

powers that are especially necessary in modern war. However narrow the intentions of the framers in granting the President the command of the armed forces, an intention that carried over into the limited views of such authorities as Hamilton and Taney, the nature of modern war has added an entirely new element to this authority: the power to wage the "war at home"—to regulate labor-management relations, commandeer plants and whole industries, control the production of munitions and distribution of necessities, sequester enemy property, reorganize the administration, even initiate prohibition. And though he can do wonders with that simple phrase "He shall be Commander in Chief," [44] he needs the support of Congress to bring the home front to the proper pitch of production and co-operation.

Congress has rarely been known to refuse this support. No less concerned with getting on with the war than the President, it has been no less eager to wield its own huge accumulation of constitutional war powers in the grand manner. The fact that the President, both as chief execu-

[44] On the special problem of the President's right as commander in chief to issue "rules and regulations" for the government of the armed forces—a power that, to judge from the famed "Lieber's Code" (General Orders, No. 100, *Official Records, War of Rebellion,* ser. III, vol. III; April 24, 1863), is hardly less sweeping than that of Congress "to make rules for the government and regulation of the land and naval forces"—see *U.S. v. Eliason,* 16 Peters 291, 301–302 (1842); *Kurtz v. Moffitt,* 115 U.S. 485,503 (1885); *Smith v. Whitney,* 116 U.S. 167 (1886). Congress has granted the President wide power to issue regulations, and these, the Court has held, have the "force of law." See *Gratiot v. U.S.,* 4 Howard 80, 117 (1846). On the distinction between regulations issued under constitutional and under legislative authority, see *Matter of Smith,* 28 Ct. Cls. 452, 459 (1888), and cases there cited. See also 6 *O.A.G.* 10.

tive and as commander in chief, controls the execution of the far-reaching laws that accompany each war, and therefore gains new strength almost every time Congress exercises its powers, gives the legislators only temporary pause. While the pages of the *Congressional Record* fill up with cries of "dictator!" "despot!" and "one-man government!" the pages of the *United States Statutes* fill up even faster with grants of authority—to seize factories, draft men, fix prices, raise money—that make him, at least in theory, all those things and a great deal more. The scope of this transfer of power can be perceived in volume 12 or 40 or 55 of the *United States Statutes*.

Inevitably, Americans being Americans even (or especially) in time of war, the authority of Congress to grant these powers, and of the President to make use of them, has been heavily challenged in a multitude of lawsuits during and after each of our three great wars. Once again the Court has been offered several excellent opportunities to call President and Congress to task and put an effective check upon the former in his often arbitrary activities as commander in chief. And once again it must be recorded that the Court has seized few, if any. For one thing, the Court, too, likes to win wars, and especially in the twentieth century has been quick to recognize the cogency of Hughes's remark that "we have a *fighting* constitution." For another, the difficulties of the judicial process and the calculated reluctance of the executive to push doubtful suits to a final decision keep many questionable laws out of the courts while the war rages, and after it as well. Thus, for example, there were no major tests of the controversial Conscription, Habeas Corpus, and Legal Tender Acts during the Civil War. The Overman Act of 1918 and the Lend-Lease Act of 1941 were likewise never challenged in the courts, principally because it was virtually impossible to raise a justiciable issue over them. And, third, whenever presented directly with the question of the validity of a wartime statute, the Court has somehow found a technical reason to avoid a straight-out ruling or, forced willy-nilly to rule, has stretched the Constitution to cover the law. All this has meant simply another vast increase in presidential power over which the Court has been unable or unwilling to exercise any real control. A brief review of the important cases is in order.

The Civil War. The two most controversial grants of power to come in due course to the Supreme Court for judgment were the Confiscation Acts of 1861 and 1862 [45] and the Legal Tender Acts of 1862.[46] The former were given approval and wide application in about thirty cases spread over ten or twelve years, the most important of which were *Miller v. United States* and *Stewart v. Kahn.*[47] The latter were brought squarely before the Court in the midst of the war in the interesting case *Roosevelt v. Meyer;* [48] but the canny justices, a majority of whom unquestionably regarded this law as beyond the financial or war powers of Congress, announced that they lacked jurisdiction, relying upon a very narrow construction of section 25 of the Judiciary Act of 1789.[49] Only Justice

[45] 12 *Stat.* 319, 589. See also 12 *Stat.* 820.

[46] 12 *Stat.* 345, 370. See also 12 *Stat.* 259, 338, 352, 532, 709.

[47] 11 Wallace 268, 304–307 (1870); 11 Wallace 493, 506–507 (1870).

[48] 1 Wallace 512 (1863).

[49] Eight years later the Court acknowledged this construction to have been in error, in *Trebilcock v. Wilson,* 12 Wallace 687, 692–694 (1871).

Nelson was prepared to meet the greenback question squarely. With the war safely past, the Court, much to its sorrow, again listened to arguments on the Legal Tender Acts, and on February 7, 1870, in *Hepburn v. Griswold* [50] held 4–3 that the recent attempt to make legal tender of paper currency had, among other faults, not been "an appropriate and plainly adapted means for carrying on war." Fifteen months and two new justices later this decision was reversed in *Knox v. Lee* [51] by a 5–4 vote, the majority opinion of Justice Strong (one of the new men) according a remarkable scope to the war powers of Congress. The less said of this unhappy incident the better for the memory of Ulysses S. Grant and a number of others, but it should be noted that the man who delivered the majority opinion in *Hepburn v. Griswold* and stuck to his guns in *Knox v. Lee,* Chief Justice Chase, had in 1862 as Secretary of the Treasury reluctantly agreed that Congress must pass this act as a much-needed spur to the war effort! His peroration on the act of 1862 is worth hearing:

It is not surprising that amid the tumult of the late civil war, and under the influence of apprehensions for the safety of the Republic almost universal, different views, never before entertained by American statesmen or jurists, were adopted by many. The time was not favorable to considerate reflection upon the constitutional limits of legislative or executive authority. If power was assumed from patriotic motives, the assumption found ready justification in patriotic hearts. . . . Not a few who then insisted upon its necessity, or acquiesced in that view, have, since the return of peace, and under the influence of the calmer time, reconsidered their conclusions,

[50] 8 Wallace 603, 617–622 (1870).
[51] 12 Wallace 457, 540–541 (1872).

and now concur in those which we have just announced. These conclusions seem to us to be fully sanctioned by the letter and spirit of the Constitution.[52]

Is it possible that we have one Constitution in peace and another in war?

World War I. The major grants of power in the first of the total wars were the Selective Service Act of 1917, Emergency Shipping Fund Act of 1917, Food and Fuel Control (Lever) Act of 1917, Trading with the Enemy Act of 1917, Railway Control Act of 1918, Executive Co-ordination (Overman) Act of 1918, Control of Communications Act of 1918, and War-Time Prohibition Act of 1918.[53] All these save the Overman Act had one or more days in the Supreme Court. The challenges to the validity of the Trading with the Enemy Act and the Railway and Communications Acts were hardly brisk, and the constitutionality of these acts was assumed virtually without argument in the important cases in which the Court construed their application.[54] The War-Time Prohibition Act was upheld strongly in *Hamilton v. Kentucky Distilleries,* less forcefully in *Ruppert v. Caffey,* two cases discussed earlier in this book.[55]

A huge but altogether justifiable grant of power was

[52] 8 Wallace 625.

[53] Respectively, 40 *Stat.* 76, 182, 276, 411, 451, 556, 904, 1046.

[54] Respectively, *Central Union Trust Co. v. Garvan,* 254 U.S. 554 (1921); *Northern Pacific Railway Co. v. North Dakota,* 250 U.S. 135, 148–150 (1919), a powerful statement of the "complete and undivided character" of the "war power of the United States" and its dominance over the rights of the states; *Dakota Central Tel. Co. v. South Dakota,* 250 U.S. 163, 183 (1919).

[55] 251 U.S. 146 (1919); 251 U.S. 264 (1920). See above, pp. 82–86.

approved with dispatch in *Arver v. United States*, the case in which Chief Justice White, announcing the judgment of a unanimous court that the Selective Draft Law of 1917 was a valid exercise of the war power, dispelled once and for all time the notion that there is something inherently unconstitutional, or perhaps extraconstitutional, about drafting men to fight our wars.[56] The law was attacked on about a dozen counts, stretching all the way from the First to the Thirteenth Amendment, but was deftly defended by the old soldier of the Confederacy. This was an outstanding instance of a case that the Court could not possibly have decided any other way, but in which it was important and altogether proper for the Court to speak in stentorian tones and give unanimous expression to the national will. In so doing it approved a war statute delegating unparalleled discretionary authority to the President, who in both our twentieth-century wars has raised armies pretty largely on his own terms.

The Emergency Shipping Fund Act of 1917 was an astounding wartime intrusion upon private interests, remarkable alike in the power asserted by Congress and in that granted the President. It authorized him virtually to

[56] 40 *Stat.* 76; 245 U.S. 366 (1918). See also *Cox v. Wood*, 247 U.S. 3 (1918), on the power of Congress to draft men to fight overseas; *McKinley v. U.S.*, 249 U.S. 397 (1919), on its power to protect the health and morals of the armies it raises, especially against "houses of ill fame, brothels, or bawdy houses." The Conscription Act of 1863 (12 *Stat.* 731) was never brought before the Supreme Court directly, but was apparently assumed to have been entirely constitutional in *U.S. v. Scott*, 3 Wallace 642 (1865); *Tarble's Case*, 13 Wallace 397, 408 (1872); *In re Grimley*, 137 U.S. 147, 153 (1890); and *Jacobson v. Massachusetts*, 197 U.S. 11, 29 (1905). An important state case upholding conscription in the Civil War was *Kneedler v. Lane*, 45 Penn. St. 238 (1863).

take over the shipbuilding industry in America. He could commandeer any yards or facilities, purchase ships at what he considered a reasonable price (with provision for subsequent revision by the courts in the event the seller deemed it unfair), or simply contract for the building of ships by negotiation. The Court, oddly enough, although construing the act on about a dozen occasions, never had occasion to discourse on its constitutionality until two months after the start of the second World War. Then, in *United States v. Bethlehem Steel Corporation*,[57] while upholding the latter's claims in a dispute over a contract, Justice Black thought it opportune to recall some truths about the war power:

We cannot regard the Government of the United States at war as so powerless that it must seek the organization of a private corporation as a helpless suppliant. The Constitution grants to Congress power "to raise and support Armies," "to provide and maintain a Navy," and to make all laws necessary and proper to carry these powers into execution. Under this authority Congress can draft men for battle service. Its power to draft business organizations to support the fighting men who risk their lives can be no less.

Finally, the single important case in which any part of the vast body of regulatory legislation enacted in World War I was held unconstitutional should be briefly mentioned. In *United States v. Cohen Grocery Co.*[58] the Court, dividing 6–2 on the constitutional question, invalidated

[57] 315 U.S. 289, 303–305 (1942).

[58] 255 U.S. 81 (1921). See also *Weeds, Inc. v. U.S.*, 255 U.S. 109 (1921); but see, too, *Highland v. Russell Car Co.*, 279 U.S. 253 (1929).

several lines of section 4 of the Lever Act,[59] which had made it "unlawful for any person wilfully . . . to make any unjust or unreasonable rate or charge in handling or dealing in or with any necessaries," as contrary to certain safeguards of the Fifth and Sixth Amendments, especially in that they failed to set up "an ascertainable standard of guilt." This was hardly a blow to presidential power. For one thing, there had never been any concerted attempt to enforce these provisions of the Lever Act, the words in question being little more than hortatory. For another, the date of this decision was February 28, 1921, and three days later Congress terminated the act and many others by joint resolution.[60] There were many brave words about the tenacity of the Fifth and Sixth Amendments in time of war, but the effects of the decision were negligible.

In a word, the Constitution was altogether equal to our first great foreign war.

World War II. In the matter of presidential use of delegated power the recent conflict followed rather closely the pattern of the first World War. At some points—price control, rationing, rent control, plant seizures, priorities— the powers cut a little deeper into the lives and economy of the people; at other points—communications, railroads, prosecutions for treasonous or obstructive speech—the government's touch was lighter. At no point did the Court find fault with the laws themselves and only rarely with their use.

Judicial battle lines were drawn between the adminis-

[59] 40 *Stat.* 276, 277, as amended by 41 *Stat.* 297, 298, attaching penalties.

[60] 41 *Stat.* 1359.

tration and private interests over only one prominent statute. In three major and several additional minor engagements the Supreme Court doggedly defended the Emergency Price Control Act of January 30, 1942,[61] against a host of outraged businessmen and landlords. The attack upon the constitutionality of the act was launched with the aid of those time-honored weapons with which war statutes are always belabored: the principle forbidding delegation of legislative power, and the Fifth Amendment. In *Yakus v. United States* the price-fixing authority of OPA was held to be a valid exercise of the war powers; [62] in *Bowles v. Willingham* rent control was likewise found constitutional.[63] And in *Steuart and Brothers v. Bowles* [64] the highhanded practice of "indirect sanctions," through which the President aided OPA, WPB, NWLB, and the rest to enforce their orders by resorting to his powers under other statutes,[65] was looked upon, if not with equanimity, at least with tolerance. In this in-

[61] 56 *Stat.* 23.

[62] 321 U.S. 414 (1944).

[63] 321 U.S. 503 (1944). See also *Lockerty v. Phillips,* 319 U.S. 182 (1943), on the power of Congress to withdraw equity jurisdiction to restrain the enforcement of OPA regulations and orders from all other courts, state or federal, except the Emergency Court of Appeals set up in the Price Control Act. Rent control was confined to much narrower limits in World War I, yet barely escaped being declared unconstitutional in *Block v. Hirsh,* 256 U.S. 135 (1921), and *Marcus Brown Co. v. Feldman,* 256 U.S. 170 (1921). In *Chastleton Corp. v. Sinclair,* 264 U.S. 543 (1924), the Court decided that the emergency had passed, and refused to enforce a 1922 extension of the 1919 District of Columbia Rent Act.

[64] 322 U.S. 398 (1944).

[65] And to his constitutional powers and prestige as well. See J. L. O'Brian and M. Fleischmann, "The War Production Board," *George Washington Law Review,* XIII (1944), 1–60.

stance the President had delegated to OPA the power given him in the Second War Powers Act of 1942 to "allocate" materials to "promote the national defense." [66] The latter had used this power to withhold scarce fuel oil from a retail dealer found guilty of loose practice in the matter of ration coupons, thereby using the authority of one act to punish him for violating regulations issued under another. This was obviously a far easier and cleaner way to deal with people who disregarded OPA regulations than the attempt to get a conviction for misdemeanor, as authorized in the Price Control Act itself. In refusing to interfere with this summary method of penalizing the Steuart Company, the Court acquiesced in an exercise of presidential war power that would seem to have infinite and explosive possibilities. And in approving, in the Yakus case, a novel and summary technique for enforcing administrative orders, it virtually abdicated its responsibility for defending the whole pattern of due process against wartime encroachment by such agencies as OPA.

Concerning the other major statutes of World War II there is little to record. In the joint resolutions declaring war against Japan, Germany, and Italy, Congress "authorized and directed" the President "to employ the entire naval and military forces of the United States and the resources of the Government to carry on" the war,[67] and this sweeping mandate was supported with some remarkable delegations of power. Few were attacked; all were held constitutional, often without so much as a word of opinion. Typical was the Court's handling of the Selective

[66] 56 *Stat.* 176, 178, 180; 7 *Fed. Reg.* 2719.

[67] 55 *Stat.* 795–797. This formula was borrowed from the declaration of war of April 6, 1917. 40 *Stat.* 1.

Service Act of 1940.[68] Although the draft was attacked and defended on constitutional grounds in many lower-court cases, the Supreme Court refused to add a single word to White's great opinion in *Arver v. United States*. A petition for certiorari to review an important lower-court case was denied without opinion.[69]

These few examples should be proof enough that in time of war Congress can pass just about any law it wants as a "necessary and proper" accessory to the delegated war powers; that the President can make just about any use of such law he sees fit; and that the people with their overt or silent resistance, not the Court with its power of judicial review, will set the only practical limits to arrogance and abuse. And as if these examples were not enough, two other handy congressional weapons have yet to be mentioned. Neither has been employed for some years now, but certainly could be dusted off quickly in case of need; each has obvious uses in these troubled times. One, congressional authorization to the President to fight a "limited war," was upheld as long ago as 1800, in a notable case arising from the French Spoliations, *Bas v. Tingy*.[70] The

[68] 54 *Stat.* 885.

[69] *Brooks v. U.S.*, 324 U.S. 878 (1945); 147 Fed. 2d 134 (1945). See also *Weightman v. U.S.*, 142 Fed. 2d 188 (1944); *Heflin v. Sanford,* 142 Fed. 2d 798 (1944). The Act of 1940 was assumed by the Supreme Court to be constitutional in dozens of cases, for example *Bowles v. U.S.*, 319 U.S. 33 (1943); *Bartchy v. U.S.*, 319 U.S. 484 (1943); *Falbo v. U.S.*, 320 U.S. 549 (1944); *Billings v. Truesdell,* 321 U.S. 542 (1944).

[70] 4 Dallas 37 (1800), seriatim opinions by Justices Moore, Washington, Chase, and Paterson approving the acts of May 28, June 13, 25, 28, and July 9, 1798, and February 9 and March 3, 1799 (1 *Stat.* 561, 565, 572, 574, 578, 613, and 743), under all of which the naval war with France was fought. See also *Talbot v. Seeman,* 1 Cranch 1, 28 (1801). The joint resolution of April 22,

other, the so-called indemnity act, through which Congress protects executive and military officials from suits for illegal actions taken in an emergency, came into prominence during and after the Civil War. The normal method was to make any order of the President or of someone acting under his authority "a defense in all courts." The omnibus provision in section four of the Habeas Corpus Act of March 3, 1863, found judicial approval in terms that made plain the Court's conviction that Congress could ratify any action that it could have authorized in the first place.[71]

Whether Congress could protect someone who acted illegally under a presidential order when it could *not* have authorized the action itself seems doubtful, but it is a matter of record that the indemnity acts of May 11, 1866, and March 2, 1867, designed to protect officers who had executed the Lincoln-Stanton program against disloyalty (in other words, designed to discourage suits based on *Ex parte Milligan*), were assumed to be constitutional by the Court in several cases.[72] And since we are entitled to assume from past performances that the Court regards the war powers of Congress as limited only by the necessities

---

1914 (38 *Stat.* 770), declaring Wilson's use of troops at Vera Cruz justified but disclaiming any purpose to make war, was one example of this power. E. S. Corwin, *Total War and the Constitution* (New York, 1947), 29, describes the Lend-Lease Act of 1941 as "to all intents and purposes . . . a qualified declaration of war."

[71] 12 *Stat.* 755, 756. *Mitchell v. Clark*, 110 U.S. 633, 640 (1884).

[72] 14 *Stat.* 46, 432. *Bean v. Beckwith*, 18 Wallace 510 (1873); *Beard v. Burts*, 95 U.S. 434 (1877); *Beckwith v. Bean*, 98 U.S. 266 (1879). For a third example of Congress' power to intervene decisively in support of executive emergency power, see *Wilson v. New*, 243 U.S. 332 (1917).

of the case, which are for Congress to ascertain, there is apparently nothing the President cannot do *constitutionally* if war should strike the country. This puts him in a position hardly less favorable than that of the Prime Minister of Great Britain, who in time of emergency can do anything that Parliament will subsequently approve. The indemnity act may be due for a revival.

The President's Authority over Courts-Martial and Military Commissions

The President is the fountainhead of military justice. As commander in chief he could not be otherwise, and Congress, in enacting and re-enacting the complexity of regulations that govern the conduct of all persons in the armed forces, has always recognized that he was, in effect, the supreme court of military law. With the normal enforcement of the newly enacted Uniform Code of Military Justice,[73] which consolidates and revises the Articles of War and the Articles for the Government of the Navy, he has little concern. Naturally he is required to take action only in important matters. For example, Article 71 of the new Code provides that a sentence of death or one "involving a general or flag officer" must be approved by him before it can be carried into execution. Article 22 authorizes him to appoint general courts-martial, a provision that, in the light of his status as commander in chief, would appear to be merely declaratory of an existing power. In these various ways Congress has recognized and

[73] *P.L.* 506, 81st Congress, 2nd session; to take effect May 31, 1951. For a blistering attack on the underlying assumptions of this code, see A. J. Keeffe and M. Moskin, "Codified Military Injustice," *Cornell Law Quarterly*, XXXV (1949), 151–170.

confirmed the primary position of the President in the system of military justice. And it should always be remembered that his pardoning power extends to every cranny of this intricate system.

The relationship between the courts-martial and the regular federal courts is extremely tenuous. The latter have always acknowledged that the courts-martial were part of an entirely different system of law. The Court has stated that a member of the armed forces belongs to a "separate community recognized by the Constitution." [74] If there is any one rule to which the civil courts have held, it is that they have no general power to review the proceedings and sentences of courts-martial.

With the sentences of courts martial which have been convened regularly, and have proceeded legally, and by which punishments are directed, not forbidden by law, . . . civil courts have nothing to do, nor are they in any way alterable by them. If it were otherwise, the civil courts would virtually administer the rules and articles of war, irrespective of those to whom that duty and obligation has been confided by the laws of the United States, from whose decisions no appeal or jurisdiction of any kind has been given to the civil magistrates or civil courts.[75]

[74] *Carter v. McLaughry*, 183 U.S. 365, 390 (1902).

[75] *Dynes v. Hoover*, 20 Howard 65, 82 (1857). For similar statements, see *Wales v. Whitney*, 114 U.S. 564, 570 (1885); *Kurtz v. Moffitt*, 115 U.S. 487, 500 (1885); *Carter v. Roberts*, 177 U.S. 496, 498 (1900). For recent indications of the continued viability of this doctrine, see *Wade v. Hunter*, 337 U.S. 684 (1949); *Humphrey v. Smith*, 337 U.S. 695 (1949); *Hiatt v. Brown*, 70 S. Ct. 495, decided March 13, 1950. For other instructive cases on the relationship of military and civil law, see *Coleman v. Tennessee*, 97 U.S. 509, 512–514 (1878); *Ex parte Mason*, 105 U.S. 696, 699–700 (1881); *Smith v. Whitney*, 116 U.S. 167, 175–186 (1886);

At the same time, even in this broad statement of non-intervention there appear certain qualifications, one might say descriptions, of those circumstances under which the civil courts would take jurisdiction of a soldier's plea for justice. The occasions for intervention have been best expressed in a noted opinion in the Court of Claims by that remarkable judge, Charles C. Nott:

The proceedings of these military tribunals cannot be reviewed in the civil courts. No writ of error will lie to bring up the rulings of a court-martial. . . . When the record of a court-martial comes into a civil court in a collateral way, the only questions which can be considered may be reduced to these three: First, was the court-martial legally constituted; second, did it have jurisdiction of the case; third, was the sentence duly approved and authorized by law.[76]

And through these narrow openings the Supreme Court has peered occasionally at the legality or jurisdiction of a court-martial. In a number of these cases some aspect of the President's position as chief dispenser of military justice has been under scrutiny, but rarely if ever has that position been challenged or impaired. Indeed, the Court, feeling somewhat shamefaced for allowing itself to be dragged by the heels into heathen territory, has excused

---

Johnson v. Sayre, 158 U.S. 109, 118 (1895); *Grafton v. U.S.*, 206 U.S. 333, 351–352 (1907); *Franklin v. U.S.*, 216 U.S. 559, 567–568 (1910); *Caldwell v. Parker*, 252 U.S. 376, 385–388 (1920); *Collins v. McDonald*, 258 U.S. 416, 418 (1922); and the important World War II case (important for draftees, at any rate) *Billings v. Truesdell*, 321 U.S. 542 (1944).

[76] *Swaim v. U.S.*, 28 Ct. Cls. 173, 217 (1893). See also *Wise v. Withers*, 3 Cranch 331, 337 (1806); *Ex parte Watkins*, 3 Peters 193, 208 (1830); *Keyes v. U.S.*, 109 U.S. 336, 340 (1883); *In re Grimley*, 137 U.S. 147, 150 (1890); *Givens v. Zerbst*, 255 U.S. 11, 19 (1921).

104

its presence by unnecessarily low bows in the direction of the commander in chief. The usual outcome of one of these cases has been to strengthen the President's hand. Thus, for example, in *Martin v. Mott* [77] the Court granted conclusive discretion to the President and his officers in such matters as fixing the number of officers, between the statutory limits of five and thirteen, for any particular court-martial; in *Swaim v. United States* [78] it spoke in approving terms of the inherent constitutional authority of the President to convene a general court-martial "in the absence of legislation expressly prohibitive"; and in a series of cases it cut the heart out of the only decision in which it had ever attempted to restrict the President, *Runkle v. United States.* [79] In that case the Court had interpreted the old sixty-fifth Article of War, which required presidential confirmation of a sentence cashiering an officer, to mean his personal approval, to be shown affirmatively on the record. In *United States v. Page, United States v. Fletcher,* and *Bishop v. United States* [80] it was announced, in effect, that he could turn over this duty to the Secretaries of War or Navy. In such case, their actions were presumed to be his in contemplation of law.

The refusal of the Court to interfere with the President's

[77] 12 Wheaton 19, 34–35 (1827). See also *Mullan v. U.S.,* 140 U.S. 240, 245 (1891).

[78] 165 U.S. 553, 558 (1897). See also 15 *O.A.G.* 290, 297–303.

[79] 122 U.S. 543, 556–560 (1887). In *McLaughry v. Deming,* 186 U.S. 49 (1902), the Court held illegal the trial of an "officer of volunteers" by a court-martial composed entirely of regular officers—something it would not do today.

[80] 137 U.S. 673, 679–680 (1891); 148 U.S. 84, 88–89 (1893); 197 U.S. 334, 341–342 (1905). For another case in which the President and his subordinates were accorded considerable latitude by the Court, see *Ex parte Reed,* 100 U.S. 13, 22–23 (1879).

activities in the area of military justice was most vividly illustrated in *Swaim v. United States*,[81] something of a *cause célèbre* of the Arthur administration. This litigation was especially interesting in that the President was involved in it just about as deeply as a President could be. The facts are these: David G. Swaim was appointed Judge Advocate General of the Army on February 22, 1881, with the rank of brigadier general. Accused of fraud and improper dealings with a banking firm in Washington, he was tried by a general court-martial convened by the President in November, 1884. Found guilty of "conduct unbecoming an officer and a gentleman," he was sentenced to be suspended from "rank, duty, and pay for three years." Dissatisfied with this sentence, which he believed not "commensurate with the offenses as found by the court," President Arthur returned the record to the general court-martial. A new sentence, suspension for one year and reduction to the rank of major, was fixed, and was likewise found unsatisfactory by the President, principally because it would require a new appointment to office. This time the court-martial did its best to please the President by sentencing Swaim to twelve years' suspension on half pay. Arthur found this, too, a stupid performance, and said as much publicly, but finally approved it "for the public interest that the proceedings in this case be not without result." After brooding over his fate for several years, and having seen Chester Alan Arthur go to his grave, Swaim at length brought suit in the Court of Claims for back pay, on the grounds that the general court-martial had been unlawfully constituted and that he had been unlawfully

[81] 165 U.S. 553 (1897), on appeal from 28 Ct. Cls. 173 (1893).

tried and sentenced. Rebuffed by that court, he took an appeal to the Supreme Court.

The Court, speaking through Justice Shiras, took up his contentions one by one, punctured them neatly, and decided unanimously for the United States. It may be instructive to set out his contentions and the Court's rejoinders:

SWAIM: The President had no power to appoint a general court-martial when my commander was not the accuser. SHIRAS: His power to appoint general courts-martial cannot be hedged in by technicalities, especially when he probably has an inherent power to convene such courts.

SWAIM: The President, by his order appointing the court-martial, became himself the accuser. SHIRAS: "Wholly unfounded."

SWAIM: The court-martial was constituted in violation of the seventy-ninth Article of War, which provides that "officers shall be tried only of general courts-martial; and no officer shall, when it can be avoided, be tried by officers inferior to him in rank." A majority of the court-martial was composed of officers inferior to me in rank. SHIRAS: "The presumption must be that the President, in detailing the officers named to compose the court-martial, acted in pursuance of law." The President had his reasons, and this Court cannot search for them.

SWAIM: One of the officers on the court-martial was of known hostility to me. SHIRAS: The decision of the court-martial to seat this officer despite challenge cannot be reviewed by a civil court in a collateral action.

SWAIM: The judge advocate was not appointed by the convening officer, nor was he sworn in; evidence for the

United States was improperly received; evidence in my behalf was improperly barred. SHIRAS: Such matters are questions of procedure and cannot be attacked in a civil court.

SWAIM: The facts did not support the conviction. SHIRAS: We cannot review.

SWAIM: The action of the President in twice returning the proceedings and urging a more severe sentence was "without authority of law." SHIRAS (in effect): Since it is not specified how many times he may do this, he may apparently do it as many times as he sees fit. And finally:

As we have reached the conclusion that the court-martial in question was duly convened and organized, and that the questions decided were within its lawful scope of action, it would be out of place for us to express any opinion on the propriety of the action of that court in its proceedings and sentence. If, indeed, as has been strenuously urged, the appellant was harshly dealt with, and a sentence of undue severity was finally imposed, the remedy must be found elsewhere than in the courts of law.[82]

This summary makes clear the two important principles adhered to consistently by the Supreme Court in cases of this type: (1) if a court-martial is legally constituted, has jurisdiction of the accused [83] and the offense, and awards a sentence authorized by law, which is then duly approved, it exists in another world from the regular courts;

[82] 165 U.S. 566. In 1894 Cleveland finally gave in to Swaim's importunities, appointed him Judge Advocate General, and retired him immediately with the rank of brigadier general.

[83] For a recent, newsworthy case in which the Supreme Court held that a court-martial lacked jurisdiction over the accused, or at least over the offense with which he had been charged, see *Hirshberg v. Cooke*, 336 U.S. 210 (1949).

(2) the exercise of discretion by the President as the fountainhead of military justice is not to be questioned in the courts of the United States.

So much for courts-martial. But there is another type of military tribunal that the President may institute, the so-called military commission, which has been characterized by a leading authority as "merely an instrumentality for the more efficient execution of the laws of war." [84] As such, the military commission is wholly the creature of the commander in chief or of one of his ranking officers in the field. Congress, too, may occasionally authorize the establishment of military commissions, as the southern states learned in the period of Reconstruction. In general, however, they are executive creations. Their jurisdiction, composition, procedure, and powers are for the President alone to determine and supervise. One use of this extraordinary type of military court was held unconstitutional in *Ex parte Milligan*. Another use is for the summary trial of civilians indicted for crimes in conquered areas. Still another is for the trial, when trial is thought at all necessary, of captured spies and enemy combatants accused of violating the laws of war.

The employment of a military commission is thus an exercise of command, hardly open to collateral attack in the civil courts of the United States, and for that matter rarely attacked. Nevertheless, there have been three outstanding uses of this type of tribunal, two of them under direct order of the President, upon which the courts have been asked to look with disfavor. The facts of these trials

[84] William Winthrop, *Abridgement of Military Law* (Washington, 1887), 330. See generally the same author's *Military Law*, II, 57–82.

and the general lesson to be drawn from them should be briefly stated.

Easily the most spectacular of all military commissions was the tribunal of nine officers authorized by President Johnson May 1, 1865, to try the assassins of Abraham Lincoln.[85] Concerning this trial and the intervention of the regular courts in its notoriously irregular proceedings there is practically nothing to say, which for our purposes is the most important fact about it. Brought to life by the President in an exercise of pure constitutional authority, the commission was based on the overwhelming conviction of an outraged people that, in the words of one of the commission's chief defenders, "The assassination of ABRAHAM LINCOLN was a military crime. While actually in command of the national forces, he was killed in a city which was his headquarters, strongly fortified and garrisoned, with a military governor. . . . Not only was the murdered commander-in-chief, to use the words of the Constitution, *in actual service in time of war,* but it was a time of *public danger.* " [86] The specification drawn up by Judge Advocate General Holt never mentioned "Abraham Lincoln, President of the United States" without adding "and Commander-in-Chief of the Army and Navy thereof."

[85] Richardson, *Messages and Papers of the Presidents,* VI, 334–335. Attorney General Speed's approval is recorded in 11 *O.A.G.* 297. For the facts and fancies of this melodrama, see Benn Pittman, compiler (and expurgator!), *The Assassination of President Lincoln* (Cincinnati, 1865); D. M. DeWitt, *The Assassination of Abraham Lincoln* (New York, 1909), and *The Judicial Murder of Mary E. Surratt* (New York, 1895); Ben: Perley Poore, *The Conspiracy Trial,* 2 vols. (Boston, 1865–1866); T. M. Harris, *The Assassination of Lincoln* (Boston, 1892).

[86] Poore, *op. cit.,* I, 3.

From start to finish this was a military trial. It was never seriously considered that it could be anything else. No civil court ever looked into the commission's authority, composition, jurisdiction, proceedings, or sentences. Under the circumstances no court could have been expected to raise its voice.

One bold attempt to gain civil justice was made in behalf of Mrs. Mary E. Surratt. At 3:00 A.M. of the day set for execution, July 7, 1865, Judge Andrew Wylie of the Supreme Court of the District of Columbia was persuaded by her counsel to issue a writ of habeas corpus to Major General W. S. Hancock, who as Commanding Officer of the Middle Military Division had custody of the doomed prisoners. At 11:30 A.M. General Hancock, accompanied by the Attorney General, surprised the skeptics by appearing before Judge Wylie. Acknowledging with respect the serving of the writ, he nonetheless declined to produce Mrs. Surratt. His authority for refusal was unimpeachable, for endorsed upon the writ were these words:

To Major General W. S. Hancock, Commander, etc.

I, ANDREW JOHNSON, President of the United States, do hereby declare that the writ of habeas corpus has been heretofore suspended in such cases as this, and I do hereby especially suspend this writ, and direct that you proceed to execute the order heretofore given upon the judgement of the Military Commission, and you will give this order in return to this writ.

Signed, ANDREW JOHNSON, President

With regret but discretion Judge Wylie gave way: "The jurisdiction of this court yields to the suspension of the writ of habeas corpus from the President of the

111

United States." Two hours later Mrs. Surratt was dead.[87]

After the decision in *Ex parte Milligan* the unfortunate Dr. Samuel Mudd, from his cell at the Dry Tortugas, applied for a writ of habeas corpus to Wayne and Chase. Mudd and the three other surviving culprits had been purposely sent to that faraway prison because Stanton, so Gideon Welles reported in his priceless diary, thought it "best to get them into a part of the country where old Nelson or any other judge would not try to make difficulty by *habeas corpus*." [88] The Chief Justice denied the writ on the ground that he had no power to issue it outside his own circuit.[89] The pardoning of the three surviving accomplices in 1869 put an end to any possibility that the legality of this military commission would ever be tested in the courts. Whether it was legal or not is now of little significance. What is significant is that in April, 1865, the military commission seemed to almost all men the natural way to deal with Booth's gang, and that when a lone judge dared to intervene, public opinion approved overwhelmingly the personal suspension of the writ of habeas corpus by the President of the United States. The Supreme Court, incidentally, was not in session, but several justices were present in Washington. Also incidentally, the two other presidential assassins, Czogolz and Guiteau, got their due from civil courts.

Three wars and seventy-seven years later, July 2, 1942, Franklin D. Roosevelt issued a proclamation appointing a military commission of seven members to try the well-

[87] See the lurid account of this last day in the *New York Times*, July 8, 1865, 1.

[88] *Diary of Gideon Welles* (Boston, 1911), II, 334.

[89] Warren, *The Supreme Court*, II, 443–444.

112

remembered "Nazi Saboteurs" for offenses against "the law of war and the Articles of War," and fixing various procedures to be followed by the commission. In a simultaneous proclamation he declared that enemy adherents apprehended in the act of entering the United States "to commit sabotage, espionage, hostile or warlike acts" were to be tried by military courts and denied access to the civil courts.[90] In all this he acted "by virtue of the authority vested in me as President and as Commander in Chief of the Army and Navy, under the Constitution and statutes of the United States, and more particularly the Thirty-Eighth Article of War." This article gave the President a general power to prescribe procedures for military courts.[91]

The saboteurs had landed from a submarine in two groups, one on Long Island June 13, the other in Florida June 17, but had apparently got nowhere with their plans to blow up assorted factories and bridges when picked up in Chicago and New York within two weeks by the FBI. Their trial began in Washington July 8. On July 28, with the case closed except for arguments of counsel, the saboteurs petitioned the District Court for the District of Columbia for a writ of habeas corpus, asserting their right to be tried in a civil court. The writ was refused, but the electrifying announcement had already been made that the Supreme Court would meet in special session July 29 to hear their petitions for writs of habeas corpus. Whether the Court was willing to hear their petition as an exercise

[90] 7 *Fed. Reg.* 5103, 5101. See generally Cyrus Bernstein, "The Saboteur Trial," *George Washington Law Review*, XI (1943), 131–190; Corwin, *Total War and the Constitution*, 117–121.

[91] *United States Code*, Title 10, sec. 1059.

of original jurisdiction is a matter of speculation, for by the time (July 31) the Court handed down its judgment, an appeal had been perfected through the Circuit Court of Appeals for the District, and the case had gone thence to the Supreme Court on certiorari.

The Court's unanimous decision in *Ex parte Quirin,* delivered *per curiam,* was that the military commission had been lawfully constituted and that the saboteurs were clearly subject to its jurisdiction. The motions for leave to file petitions for writs of habeas corpus were therefore denied, the orders of the district court affirmed. The military trial resumed, the prisoners were found guilty, and on August 8 the President announced that six of the saboteurs had been electrocuted and two sentenced to long prison terms.

Not until three months later, when the Court met for its regular October term, was its reasoning made public. In an elaborate twenty-two-page opinion Chief Justice Stone took up one by one the principal contentions of counsel for the saboteurs and disposed of them with the aid of history and military law. The complexities of this opinion need not detain us.[92] It will be sufficient to our purposes to mention these few of the many points made by the Chief Justice: (1) the President's proclamation did not "preclude access to the courts for determining its applicability" to this particular case; (2) it was not necessary for the Court to discuss the President's power as commander in chief to create this commission, for Congress, in the fifteenth Article of War, had in effect "au-

[92] 317 U.S. 1 (1942). The Chief Justice's arguments are neatly summarized in R. E. Cushman, "The Case of the Nazi Saboteurs," *American Political Science Review,* XXXVI (1942), 1082–1091.

thorized trial of offenses against the law of war before such commissions"; (3) the offenses charged against the saboteurs were offenses against the law of war, which has always recognized that unlawful combatants are subject "to trial and punishment by military tribunals for acts which render their belligerency unlawful"; (4) the procedural guarantees of Amendments V and VI were never intended to apply to military trials (again the emphasis is on two separate and distinct systems of law); (5) *Ex parte Milligan* did not apply to this situation, and indeed must be confined closely to the facts under which it arose; and (6) the President could validly fix the procedures to be followed by the commission.

There have been two general estimates of the value of *Ex parte Quirin*. One opinion holds that the willingness of the Court to assemble and inspect the legality of a presidentially sponsored military trial was in itself a fact of no little moment for constitutional law and civil liberty. The prisoners did, after all, get through to the highest court in the land to have their questions answered, and the Court "stopped the military authorities and required them, as it were, to show their credentials. When this had been done to the Court's satisfaction, they were allowed to proceed." [93] The other opinion regards the Court's participation "as little more than a ceremonious detour to a predetermined goal intended chiefly for edification." [94]

The truth lies somewhere between these two extremes. Even as a solemn pageant masking the naked power of the President to have these surreptitious invaders shot on the

[93] Cushman, *loc. cit.*, 1091.
[94] Corwin, *op. cit.*, 118.

115

spot, the convocation of the Court had its good points, especially as a warning to future Presidents and military commissions to proceed in such matters in a careful way. And yet the whole affair was a shadow play without blood or substance. There was something a little pathetic about the Court's eagerness to hear the pleas of the saboteurs, and something a little odious about the comparison of the ready hearing accorded these scoundrels with the glue-footed course of justice for the Japanese-Americans and citizens of Hawaii. The brave arguments of Colonels Cassius M. Dowell and Kenneth Royall, who wrung the last drop of support out of the suffering corpse of Lambdin P. Milligan, were likewise hollow with unreality. When the Attorney General remarked, "The President's power over enemies who enter this country in time of war, as armed invaders intending to commit hostile acts, must be absolute," he had said all that was really necessary to say. And yet when asked by the Chief Justice, "Does the Attorney General challenge the jurisdiction of the Court?" Mr. Biddle replied, "I do not." In that simple exchange was summed up the total value of *Ex parte Quirin.*

From this trial to that of General Tomoyuki Yamashita was but a step, although from the point of view of judicial oversight of executive-military authority it was a step to the rear. In this instance the Court examined the authority of a military commission established in 1945 by order of General W. D. Styer, Commanding General, United States Army Forces in the Western Pacific, to try General Yamashita for offenses against the law of war, especially his failure to restrain his troops from committing atrocities

116

against Americans and Filipinos.[95] Once again the Court asserted its right to scrutinize the authority and proceedings of a military commission, and once again found them either satisfactory or unreviewable. It was upon this latter element of the majority opinion—the unreviewability of the manifestly irregular methods employed in Yamashita's trial—that Justice Rutledge seized in an elaborate dissent, and in these terms pointed directly to the logical conclusion of the majority holding:

> The difference between the Court's view of this proceeding and my own comes down in the end to the view, on the one hand, that there is no law restrictive upon these proceedings other than whatever rules and regulations may be prescribed for their government by the executive authority or the military and, on the other hand, that the provisions of the Articles of War, of the Geneva Convention and the Fifth Amendment apply.[96]

It was his belief, and Justice Murphy's as well, that the military commission had disregarded flagrantly the accepted standards of procedural due process—for example, in accepting depositions and hearsay evidence—and should have been called to task by the Supreme Court. The majority regarded the procedure and rules of evidence of a military commission as reviewable only by higher military authorities.

There would be little profit and much confusion in

[95] *In re Yamashita*, 327 U.S. 1 (1946). See generally Charles Fairman, "The Supreme Court on Military Jurisdiction," *Harvard Law Review*, LIX (1946), 866–881, and the bristling attack by A. F. Reel, *The Case of General Yamashita* (Chicago, 1949).
[96] 327 U.S. 81.

117

examining the many constitutional, moral, and interna-
tional-legal questions raised for consideration in the Yamashita case, and in the dozens of other petitions for writs
of habeas corpus on behalf of captured generals, poli-
ticians, and even privates that flooded the Court between
1946 and 1950.[97] Their lesson for this study may be very
simply phrased: The Supreme Court of the United States
cannot be expected, indeed has no right, to set itself up
as a sort of supermilitary commission to oversee the world-
wide activities of the punitive tribunals that the President
has authorized, often in conjunction with our allies, to

[97] See the excellent article of Charles Fairman, "Some New
Problems of the Constitution Following the Flag," *Stanford Law
Review*, I (1949), 587–645. The most important of these quests for
relief were: (1) *Homma v. Patterson*, 327 U.S. 759 (1946); motion for leave to file petition for writ of habeas corpus denied *per
curiam* on authority of *In re Yamashita*, with vigorous dissents by
Justices Murphy and Rutledge. (2) *Milch v. U.S.*, 332 U.S. 789
(1947); similarly disposed of, although four of the justices wanted
an argument on the jurisdiction of the Court. (3) *Hirota v. Mac-
Arthur*, 335 U.S. 876 (1948), 338 U.S. 197 (1948); with the
addition of Justice Jackson, back from Nuremberg, to the four
inquisitive judges of *Milch v. U.S.*, the Court heard arguments as
to its jurisdiction, but declared itself as "satisfied" (with Murphy
dissenting, Rutledge reserving decision, and Douglas concurring
separately) that the international tribunal set up by General Mac-
Arthur to try the Japanese war criminals was "not a tribunal of the
United States." For other citations, see Fairman, *loc. cit.*, 589n.,
591n., 594n., 600–603nn.; for an important (and consistent) recent
case, see *Johnson v. Eisentrager*, 70 S. Ct. 936, decided June 5,
1950. Though I cannot agree with, I can admire deeply, the dissenting stand of Justices Black, Douglas, and Burton. Even more
admirable was the opinion of Circuit Judge E. Barrett Prettyman,
174 Fed. 2nd 961. That this whole issue has not been decided
with finality is made plain in P. B. Perlman, "*Habeas Corpus* and
Extraterritoriality," *American Bar Association Journal*, XXXVI
(1950), 187–190, 249–252.

pursue the laws of war to their harsh but imperative conclusions. If we did commit a moral and practical blunder at Nuremberg and Tokyo and Manila, the man to correct it, if correction were even possible, is the man whom history will hold accountable, the President of the United States. What he and his commanders have done in the occupied countries they have done *politically*, in the purest sense of the word, and the trials of these alleged war criminals were part of that pattern. The brave and angry and altogether understandable protests of Justices Murphy and Rutledge notwithstanding, the Court was right in recognizing its constitutional and practical incapacity to bring justice to Yamashita, Milch, Homma, Hirota, and the rest. We can sympathize strongly with Rutledge's anxiety that trials of this sort meet the high standards of the Anglo-American legal tradition, but that, too, is for the President or Congress to decide; even an expression of national shame by the Court lies beyond the end zone of the judicial function. The trials of the war criminals are one type of "judicial" proceeding in which the standards are set and maintained by the President, not the Court. His sins the justices may lament, but not in public. This would seem to be the general rule for the Supreme Court's review and control of these extraordinary military commissions.

One final fact, just a little too curious to be relegated to a footnote: In one of these cases Colonel Willis M. Everett, Jr., chief defense counsel in the military trial at Dachau of the Germans charged with perpetrating the massacre at Malmedy, sought to file a petition in the Supreme Court for a writ of habeas corpus for Bersin, one of his clients. There was nothing unusual about this move, but in making it he named the President (as Commander-in-Chief of the Armed Forces of the United States), the Secretaries of Defense and Army, the Chief of Staff, and the Attorney General as respondents! The case, as it will be cited in the years to come, bears a President's name for the first and only time since *Mississippi v. Johnson*. It might have been *In re Bersin;* it turned out to be *Everett v. Truman!* [98]

The President's Authority over Conquered Territory

The task of governing our defeated enemies has been front-page news for more than five years. The toils and trials of Clay and McCloy in Germany, MacArthur in Japan, and Clark in Austria have captured the continuous attention of the American people. Have they captured the Court's as well? Not as a court, certainly, for our military and civil governors, acting directly as agents of the commander in chief, have been spared the necessity of justifying their activities to the Supreme Court of the United States. [99]

It was not always thus. There were times—after the Mexican War, Civil War, and Spanish-American War—

[98] 334 U.S. 824 (1948).

[99] For an informative survey of some of the problems of military government in World War II, see Charles Fairman, "Some Observations on Military Occupation," *Minnesota Law Review,* XXXII (1948), 319–348. See also C. J. Friedrich *et al., American Experiences in Military Government in World War II* (New York, 1948); Harold Zink, *American Military Government in Germany* (New York, 1947); Friedrich and Connor, eds., *Military Government* (Philadelphia, 1950).

when the Supreme Court was fairly flooded with litigation that demanded close examination of the President's powers of military government over conquered enemy territory.[100] Those were the days when American traders, and other nationals as well, could get loose in Vera Cruz or New Orleans or San Juan about one day after (if not before) the fighting had ceased, and could get involved in the most complicated squabbles with the military authorities. A disproportionate number of these came in time to the Supreme Court, which in settling them said just about everything that can be said about this interesting aspect of presidential power. No branch of his martial authority has been quite so fully explored and precisely defined. Although the chief reason for the absence of judicial oversight of our occupying activities is the absence of private interests in a position to push their suits, the fullness with which the Court has already expounded the President's powers of military government, and has given them the widest possible scope, would be enough to discourage the most gravely injured litigant. Another reason, of course, is the Court's constitutional and practical inability to oversee the joint activities of allied military government, a fact made clear in *Hirota v. MacArthur.* The condominium has no place in our constitutional law.

An unlimited number of pages might easily be devoted to the dozens of cases on this subject, especially since many of them provided the judicial climax to some rather colorful clashes between civilians at their most clever and soldiers at their most stupid. Yet all point in the same di-

[100] After the War of 1812 there were a few cases dealing with this problem in reverse. See for example *U.S. v. Rice,* 4 Wheaton 246 (1819).

rection, toward presidential autonomy, and thus may be disposed of in short order.

The central doctrine of military government, adhered to by the Court rigidly and almost with a sigh of relief, is that the President governs all conquered territory in his capacity as commander in chief, and that his determinations when an area is ready for military government,[101] what shape such government is to assume,[102] how far it is to dispossess or make use of existing law and institutions,[103] and when it is to cease [104] are conclusive and not to be questioned in any court of the United States. His powers are absolute, limited neither by the Constitution and laws of the United States nor by those of the conquered area, but only by the "laws of war." [105] Although in one of the *Insular Cases* the Court remarked of the President's military commander that "while his power is necessarily despotic, this must be understood rather in an administrative than a legislative sense," and that "his power to legislate would not be without certain restrictions—in other words, they would not extend beyond the necessities of the case" [106]—it is clear that the President

[101] *U.S. v. Pico,* 23 Howard 321 (1859); *U.S. v. Yorba,* 1 Wallace 412, 423 (1863); *Hornsby v. U.S.,* 10 Wallace 224, 239 (1869).

[102] *New Orleans v. Steamship Co.,* 20 Wallace 387, 393–394 (1874); *Dow v. Johnson,* 100 U.S. 158, 170 (1879). See also *Cross v. Harrison,* 16 Howard 164, 190 (1853); *Texas v. White,* 7 Wallace 700, 729–730 (1869).

[103] *Leitensdorfer v. Webb,* 20 Howard 176, 177–178 (1857); *Coleman v. Tennessee,* 97 U.S. 509, 517 (1878).

[104] *Neely v. Henkel,* 180 U.S. 109, 124 (1901).

[105] *Dooley v. U.S.,* 182 U.S. 22, 230–231 (1901).

[106] 182 U.S. 234. See also *Raymond v. Thomas,* 91 U.S. 712, 716 (1875), and *Lincoln v. U.S.,* 197 U.S. 419, 428 (1905), for examples of purely technical limits that the Court has occasionally

alone may judge of these necessities. It is also for him to decide how justice is to be administered—by what manner of court and under what law.[107] And certainly his orders have the force of law, superior law.[108]

Military government may be as arbitrary and absolute as the President and his commanders care to make it. He may authorize the requisitioning of private property and "exaction" of contributions from the local population, or order it, as Polk did in the Mexican War.[109] Or, if he should want to support the occupation in a more normal fashion, he may impose the necessary taxes and customs duties.[110] In any case, he governs the area in every aspect without interference from any source. His will is law, and the Court has no power to hold it in check. Several hundred cases all say the same thing, that to all intents and purposes military government under the commander in chief is "an absolutism of the most complete sort." [111]

---

set upon the actions of occupying military commanders, although hardly upon those of the President.

[107] *The Grapeshot,* 9 Wallace 129, 132–133 (1869); *Burke v. Miltenberger,* 19 Wallace 519 (1873). A technical limit is set in *Jecker v. Montgomery,* 13 Howard 498, 515 (1851).

[108] *Cross v. Harrison,* 16 Howard 164, 190 (1853).

[109] *Diary of James K. Polk* (Chicago, 1910), III, 156–157; Winthrop, *Abridgement of Military Law,* 324–325. See *Herrera v. U.S.,* 222 U.S. 558, 571–572 (1912).

[110] *Mechanics Bank v. Union Bank,* 22 Wallace 276, 295–297 (1874); *Dooley v. U.S.,* 182 U.S. 222, 231–232 (1901); *MacLeod v. U.S.,* 229 U.S. 416, 425 (1913).

[111] A. H. Carpenter, "Military Government of Southern Territory," *American Historical Association Reports,* I (1900), 496. Other important sources on military government are D. Y. Thomas, *A History of Military Government* (New York, 1904); W. E. Birkhimer, *Military Government and Martial Law* (3d ed.; Kansas City, 1914); Elihu Root, *The Military and Colonial Policy of the United States* (Cambridge, 1916).

This type of government normally extends until the withdrawal of our troops under the terms of a peace treaty or other agreement with the occupied power. If the United States is to acquire the territory permanently, the President's exclusive power of military government is considered to cease at the time of *de jure* transfer of sovereignty. The Court has several times had occasion to agree that "it is a well-recognized principle in the United States that, when a territory is annexed by the United States or comes in any manner under its jurisdiction, Congress has an absolute right, from the moment of any acquisition, to determine the political rights and governmental organization of that territory." [112] Generally, of course, Congress is not prepared to extend civil government immediately to such an area. The Court has indicated clearly the proper substitute:

The civil government of the United States cannot extend immediately and of its own force over conquered and ceded territory. Theoretically, Congress might prepare and enact a scheme of civil government to take effect immediately upon the cession, but, practically, there always have been delays and always will be. Time is required for a study of the situation and for the maturing and enacting of an adequate scheme of civil government. In the meantime, pending the action of Congress, there is no civil power under our system of government, not even that of the President as civil executive, which can take the place of the government which has ceased to exist. . . . Is it possible that, under such circumstances, there must be an interregnum? We think clearly not. The au-

[112] Berdahl, *War Powers of the Executive*, 252; *Cross v. Harrison,* 16 Howard 164, 193–195 (1853); *Downes v. Bidwell,* 182 U.S. 244, 345 (1901). See Lawson Reno, "The Power of the President to Acquire and Govern Territory," *George Washington Law Review,* IX (1941), 251–285.

thority to govern such . . . territory is found in the laws applicable to conquest and session. That authority is the military power, under the control of the President as Commander-in-Chief.[113]

Although this interesting fission of the President into two halves, one civil and the other military, is not exactly sound constitutional theory, the Court's words do give an accurate picture of his power in this field. Whether as commander in chief or as beneficiary of specific congressional authorization, he governs our permanently conquered territories for an indefinite number of years. In any event, these are matters for political, not judicial, determination. The President's powers of military government comprise a field in which the Court has done a great deal of interpreting and exercised no control, indeed has been a sort of judicial handmaiden to perfect absolutism.[114]

[113] *Santiago v. Nogueras*, 214 U.S. 260, 265 (1909).

[114] Another problem that used to agitate the Court occasionally and is now, with the arrival of total war, of purely antiquarian interest is the power of the President in the field against the enemy, especially in connection with the confiscation of enemy and requisition of friendly property. Among the cases of this type, almost all of them litigations in which the Court held for the government and against the assaults of injured private interests, are *Brown v. U.S.*, 8 Cranch 110, 122–129 (1814); *Mitchell v. Harmony*, 13 Howard 115, 132–135 (1855); *Mrs. Alexander's Cotton*, 2 Wallace 404, 418–421 (1864); *U.S. v. Padelford*, 9 Wallace 531, 540–541 (1869); *Miller v. U.S.*, 11 Wallace 268, 304–307 (1870); *U.S. v. Russell*, 13 Wallace 623 (1871); *Young v. U.S.*, 97 U.S. 39, 58–61 (1877); *U.S. v. Pacific Railroad*, 120 U.S. 227, 239 (1887); *Hijo v. U.S.*, 194 U.S. 315, 322 (1904); *Juragua Iron Co. v. U.S.*, 212 U.S. 297, 305–310 (1909), and the many cases there cited. In *Totten v. U.S.*, 92 U.S. 105 (1876), the Court upheld the power of the President to employ secret agents behind enemy lines and to make his secret promise of payment a contract binding on the government.

Conclusion

THIS discussion of the war powers of the President has already spawned so many generalizations and conclusions that there is not much left to pronounce by way of summation. Nevertheless, it might be helpful to pull together the main strands of fact and law that have appeared repeatedly in the decisions in this field. The total performance of the Court in and after our three great wars leads to these observations concerning judicial review and control of the President's actions as commander in chief:

First, the wealth of cases is somewhat misleading. Actually, the Court has been asked to examine only a tiny fraction of his significant deeds and decisions as commander in chief, for most of these were by nature challengeable in no court but that of impeachment—which was entirely as it should have been. The contours of the presidential war powers have therefore been presidentially, not judicially, shaped; their exercise is for Congress and the people, not the Court, to oversee.

Second, even when presidential or military actions work questionable inroads upon private rights and raise clearly justiciable controversies, it is extremely difficult for injured persons to obtain definitive judicial scrutiny of them, at least in time to do anyone much good. It is interesting to speculate as to which agency—the United States Army, the Department of Justice, or the Supreme Court—is most reluctant to see a highly charged presidential-military action forced through to a final decision at the law. The Army and the government lawyers apparently have no scruples about staving off an unpredictable judicial pronouncement, for we know that they will release interned prisoners and hand back seized factories the day before attorneys for these injured interests are to begin arguments in Washington. The Court in its turn will gladly agree that the case is moot, or it will seize with relief upon a technicality preventing it from taking jurisdiction, or, if forced to speak, it will decide the issue on the narrowest possible grounds. The picture is not pretty, especially when the subjects are decent and patriotic judges, soldiers, and lawyers. The explanation, of course, is that a challenge to an evacuation order or a plant seizure or a suspension of habeas corpus or an emancipation proclamation raises a question so politically explosive that the very notion of "government by lawsuit" becomes unthinkable. Whatever we allow this process to settle in peace, we cannot submit to its vagaries in time of war. The judges appear to realize this truth; perhaps in time more of them will come right out and state it.

Third, whatever limits the Court has set upon the employment of the war powers have been largely theoretical, rarely practical. Even admitting that *Ex parte Milligan, United States v. Cohen Grocery Co.*, and *Duncan v. Kahanamoku* have their uses as warnings to the political branches to fight our wars constitutionally, the warning is merely moral.[1] Future Presidents are likely to pay about

[1] The attempt to read morality into this part of the Constitution reached its zenith in Taney's opinion in *Fleming v. Page,* 9 Howard

as much attention to these decisions as did Lincoln, Wilson, and Roosevelt; the first and third were long dead, Wilson but three days from the end of his term, when the great limiting decision of each one's particular war was announced by a stern-visaged Court. Justice Burton, dissenting in the Duncan case, clearly overrated the significance of these decisions when he warned,

It is important . . . that in reviewing the constitutionality of the conduct of our agencies of government in time of war, invasion or threatened invasion, we do not now make precedents which in other emergencies may handicap the executive branch of the Government in the performance of duties allotted to it by the Constitution and by the exercise of which it successfully defended the nation against the greatest attack ever made upon it.[2]

Fourth, enough evidence is in from our three great conflicts with which to construct a definite, henceforth predictable pattern of wartime judicial review. *Bello flagrante* we may expect such performances—both good and bad, but all pointing to *power*—as the *Prize Cases, Roosevelt v. Meyer, Ex parte Vallandigham, Arver v. United States, Yakus v. United States,* and *Korematsu v. United States. Post bellum* we will hear about *limitations—Ex parte*

603, 614 (1850), in which he wrote that "the genius and character of our institutions are peaceful, and the power to declare war was not conferred upon Congress for the purposes of aggression and aggrandizement, but to enable the general government to vindicate by arms, if it should become necessary, its own rights and the rights of its citizens.

"A war, therefore, declared by Congress, can never be presumed to be waged for the purpose of conquest or the acquisition of territory."

The context of these comments was the Mexican War.

[2] 327 U.S. 357.

CONCLUSION

Milligan, Hepburn v. Griswold, United States v. Cohen Grocery Co., and *Duncan v. Kahanamoku.* We may even expect occasionally to hear the existence of this pattern frankly confessed, as it was by Davis in the Milligan case and by Chase in *Hepburn v. Griswold.*[3] There do indeed seem to be two Constitutions—one for peace, the other for war.

Fifth, the Court has had little success in preventing the precedents of war from becoming precedents of peace. We might even go so far as to say that the Court has made a positive contribution to the permanent peacetime weakening of the separation of powers, the principle of nondelegation, the Fifth Amendment, and the necessary and proper clause as applicable limits to governmental power. Certainly its decisions in *Hamilton v. Kentucky Distilleries* and *Woods v. Miller Co.,* in which it confessed its incapacity to call a halt to the postwar exercise of the war powers, have helped project the loose principles of the Constitution-at-war into present interpretations of the Constitution-at-peace. Even more certainly, the doctrine of *Ex parte Milligan* and *United States v. Cohen Grocery Co.* has actually backfired on the Court. By insisting that the two Constitutions were really only one, the Court has contributed heavily to that emphasis on the Constitution

[3] See above, pp. 37–38, 93–94. Instructive, too, are Jackson's concurring thoughts in *Woods v. Miller Co.,* 333 U.S. 138, 146 (1948): "No one will question that [the war] power is the most dangerous one to free government in the whole catalogue of powers. It usually is invoked in haste and excitement when calm legislative consideration of constitutional limitation is difficult. It is executed in a time of patriotic fervor that makes moderation unpopular. And, worst of all, it is interpreted by judges under the influence of the same passions and pressures."

as grant of power that dominates present-day constitutional law. No man ever expressed this truth more clearly than that great limitationist, Justice Field, in his mordant dissent from *Juilliard v. Greenman*,[4] in which the peacetime issuance of notes as legal tender was held constitutional: "What was in 1862 called the 'medicine of the Constitution' has now become its daily bread. So it always happens that whenever a wrong principle of conduct, political or personal, is adopted on a plea of necessity, it will be afterwards followed on a plea of convenience." It is the Court itself that has had the most trouble distinguishing medicine from bread.

Sixth, the Court appears at last to have realized this situation, and is now launched upon a long-range trend away from the fatuous indignation of *Ex parte Milligan* and toward the tough-mindedness displayed by Justices Jackson, Burton, and Frankfurter in their several opinions in *Korematsu v. United States* and *Duncan v. Kahana-moku*. Increasingly the justices are speaking and interpreting in terms of "the *fighting* Constitution," and this trend, if not carried too far, could be a welcome departure. If the Court would be a little more clear-voiced about the general power of this nation to make war, it could then turn around and deliver a great deal more relief in specific instances of individual injustice, which was all it was supposed to do in the first place. In short, the less it pretends, the more it can defend.

Seventh, the criterion of this fighting Constitution is and will be the "reasonable decision," as arrived at by that irrepressible fellow, the "reasonable man." The "allowable limits of military discretion" that the Court will tolerate

[4] 110 U.S. 421, 458 (1884).

are those that a reasonable man would have determined in the circumstances with which the defendant official was actually faced. This, of course, is a formula of practically no value for judicial review of executive-military action. It is the soldier charged with military success, on the spot and at the time, not the judge charged with dispensing justice, in the court two years later, who must determine "reasonably" the extent of the war power in any particular situation. And the ultimate identity of the "reasonable man" is, as everyone knows, the President of the United States, whom no court of law is likely to brand unreasonable.

Finally, the implications of this study for constitutional law in the atomic age should be crystal clear. As in the past, so in the future, President and Congress will fight our wars with little or no thought about a reckoning with the Supreme Court. Such major constitutional issues as the hotly contested question of the President's authority to station troops in Europe will be resolved politically, not judicially. Most important, the defense of the Constitution rests at bottom exactly where the defense of the nation rests: in the good sense and good will of the political branches of the national government, which for most martial purposes must mean the President and his military commanders. This is a sad moral to proclaim after so long a journey, but it is one that we should have firmly fixed in our constitutional understanding. In the clear, cold words of Justice Jackson:

Of course the existence of a military power resting on force, so vagrant, so centralized, so necessarily heedless of the individual, is an inherent threat to liberty. But I would not lead people to rely on this Court for a review that seems to me wholly delusive. . . . If the people ever let command of the war power fall into irresponsible and unscrupulous hands, the courts wield no power equal to its restraint. The chief restraint upon those who command the physical forces of the country, in the future as in the past, must be their responsibility to the political judgments of their contemporaries and to the moral judgments of history.[5]

[5] *Korematsu v. U.S.*, 323 U.S. 214, 248 (1944).

132

Table of Cases

Page

Index

141

143